Personal Mastery

Other Books by Dr. Moss include:

Depression Exposed: A Spiritual
Enlightenment on a Dark Subject

How to Grieve and Let Go with Dignity: A
Spiritual Handbook to Help Overcome
the Pain of Death, Divorce, or
Abandonment

Personal Mastery

The Believer's
Road Map to Destiny

Perry Moss, Jr., M.A. &
Belinda G. Moss, Ph.D.

WESTBOW
PRESS
A DIVISION OF THOMAS NELSON

WestBow Press books may be ordered through booksellers or by contacting:

WestBow Press
A Division of Thomas Nelson
1663 Liberty Drive
Bloomington, IN 47403
www.westbowpress.com
1-(866) 928-1240

Because of the dynamic nature of the Internet, any web addresses or
links contained in this book may have changed since publication and
may no longer be valid. The views expressed in this work are solely those
of the author and do not necessarily reflect the views of the publisher,
and the publisher hereby disclaims any responsibility for them.

Any people depicted in stock imagery provided by Thinkstock are
models, and such images are being used for illustrative purposes only.

Certain stock imagery © Thinkstock.

ISBN: 978-1-4497-2492-4 (sc)
ISBN: 978-1-4497-2493-1 (ebk)

Library of Congress Control Number: 2011914948

Printed in the United States of America

WestBow Press rev. date: 10/04/2011

To Our Lord and Saviour
Jesus Christ

We thank God for the privilege to impart His knowledge to the Body of Christ. It is our sincerest desire to minister the blessing of the Lord in a way that will empower God's people to rise to every occasion and provide evidence that proves that the Kingdom of God rules over all. In a world filled with turmoil, degradation, and demise, this evidence will demonstrate that the Kingdom of God is firm and stable and cannot be shaken. We not only have the solution to the world's problems, WE ARE THE SOLUTION.

This book is, therefore, dedicated to our Lord and Saviour Jesus Christ for empowering us to empower others. You led by example and we're following your lead.

We love you!

Table of Contents

Preface

❧❧

This book, Personal Mastery, is written to help believers prepare themselves to confront and defeat the unexpected challenges of life, temptations of success, and the shames of past failures by learning how to navigate through life victoriously utilizing the wisdom of God.

Personal Mastery is about practicing and acquiring skills ahead of time so that when you are confronted with adversity, what you have practiced will aid in your defense—it will fight for you; it is being sufficient for all things. It's about proofing the heart, emotions and thinking powers, to rule for you during times of conflict.

Personal Mastery is not about becoming an expert; it's about increasing in wisdom, and maintaining superior emotional stability and sustained motivation to fulfill destiny—the ultimate motivator and goal of every believer.

We have written two books on the same subject. This particular *version* is written to the Ecclesia—the called out ones—the church—Believers. It provides spiritual insight on the set time for the church to invade culture with the gifts and callings of God, but not until we learn *Personal Mastery*.

The scripture says Jesus is the desire of nations. The problem is they don't realize He is *their desire*. Consequently, we have written a similar book for the secular community, entitled, "Self-Mastery: The Art of Fulfillment." It contains the same powerful, transforming information, but without the spiritual connotations. We believe we have the answer to *the world's* problems and don't want it to be rejected because the "answer" is conveyed with a scripture and verse. The Word of God has self-fulfilling power and that power is not diminished when a scripture is not cited. Trust me, God won't be offended. Notice that He doesn't add his signature next to the sun when it rises for fear that someone else would get the credit.

The very nature of a believer is to empower others (we are blessed to be a blessing). We are not to withhold or hide vital revelation because people have not yet received Christ. How will they become believers until they hear and see the truth?

The world sometimes categorizes our books as self help or religious. However, both are wrong. We can do nothing without the Lord—not even help ourselves, and religion destroys; after all, it was religion that killed Jesus. No, our books pierce the heart. We deal with issues that face believers, issues that the religious community would rather ignore or deny that they exist in the church; yet Christians, who are the most powerful entity on the planet, are dying on the vine.

We have discovered that one of the most debilitating hindrances in the church is a lack of personal self-awareness. We have preached and taught many sermons on faith, but have neglected a critical related subject and that is the emotional state of the believer. So, we're going to take care of that with this book on *Personal Mastery*.

"Many of you have read my book entitled 'Depression Exposed, A Spiritual Enlightenment on a Dark Subject,' where I, Dr. Belinda Moss, the co-author of this book, exposed my 20-year struggle with depression that led to a life of suicide ideation and culminated with two suicide attempts. Get this, I was a tongue-talking, Bible preaching, power-packed powerhouse for God in the pulpit and a stellar Air Force Officer on the military platform, but behind closed doors, I was a mess. My bout with depression led to me placing a .357 magnum to my head, only to survive due to a malfunction with the gun."

Now, some 20 years later, we both see clearly why believers don't have the influence we should as members of the Body of Christ. It is because many believers have not dealt with the issues of their heart. Rather, many are living with past hurts, addictions, identity crises, insecurities, and more emphatically, just plain don't love themselves.

We have been studying for some time, the end-time role of the church. We have noticed that the church, the most powerful body on the planet, is ignored by the world. Few outside the four walls want to hear what we have to say. Why? Because they don't see anything "on us" that commands their attention. We have the same divorce rate, same sexual problems, same identity issues, same fears about giving, or living, etc. My goodness, you can't distinguish the believers from the non-believers. Why, because we don't understand our role as members of the Body of Christ. We have no revelatory end-time vision except from an eschatological viewpoint and as the man of wisdom says, "Where there is no vision, the people perish" (Proverbs 29:18). The literal translation of this verse is the people are made naked (of no effect).

If we are to be the end-time church to do great exploits in these last days, we can no longer sweep these matters under the rug, or bury our heads in the sand as if they don't exist. Pressures will inevitably expose what is in the heart and the accuser of the brethren—Satan has surely demonstrated that he is skilled in allowing you to get away with your mess for what seems like eternity just so the harvest can explode in your face when you least expect it.

Christ is defined as the Anointed One and His anointing. That means as members of the Body of Christ, each of us has been graced with gifts and callings to complete assignments that lead to fulfilling destiny. According to the book of Jeremiah, God has placed our face in the future (Jeremiah 1:5, 29:11) and as we align ourselves with God, like a compass, we receive direction to get us to that place of destiny.

By that same grace, this book will pierce the heart of the serious believer to take an in-depth look at their heart and examine whether they are dwelling perpetually in a kingdom state; a state of righteousness, peace and joy; a place that allows you to not only receive "strength that you need, mercy and grace," but also visions and dreams; a state where you can hear the voice of God and receive strategies to join God in what He is doing in this generation.

This is a great assignment and once you discover it, you will be both honored and humbled to be "chosen for such a time as this." This book will take you on a journey to become totally transformed in the spirit of your mind to be the true man or woman of God you were predestined to be before time began.

Although this book was written jointly by the both of us, there are sections in the book where we share our individual testimonies. To avoid confusion, we have indicated which author is speaking at that time and the narrative is in quotation marks. Now, buckle your seat-belts, this road map, if followed carefully, will place you on a fast track that is guaranteed to get your feet to where your face is in the future.

Perry & Belinda Moss
Smithfield, Virginia

❧❧

The Invitation

*"Look, you scoffers and scorners, and marvel and
perish and vanish away; for I am doing a deed
in your days, a deed which you will never have
confidence in or believe, [even] if someone [clearly
describing it in detail] declares it to you."*
Acts 13:41, AMP

What made Wayne Gretsky a phenomenal hockey
player is that he was able to capture an awareness
and strategy of the game that most of the players
missed. He said, "A **good** hockey player plays where the puck
is. A **great** hockey player plays where the puck is going to be."
Wayne Gretsky possessed the principal aspect of greatness;
he understood the game of hockey—he understood the big
picture.

What made Jesus such an exceptional Son of God is that He
always knew what the Father was doing and was bent on joining
him. Note these two revealing scriptures:

*"But Jesus answered them, My Father has worked
[even] until now, [He has never ceased working; He
is still working] and I, too, must be at [divine] work"
(John 5:17, AMP).*

> *"So Jesus answered them by saying, I assure you, most solemnly I tell you, the Son is able to do nothing of Himself (of His own accord); but He is able to do only what He sees the Father doing, for whatever the Father does is what the Son does in the same way [in His turn]. The Father dearly loves the Son and discloses to (shows) Him everything that He Himself does. And He will disclose to Him (let Him see) greater things yet than these, so that you may marvel and be full of wonder and astonishment" (John 5:19-20, AMP).*

Jesus was on to something. He was saying, He's successful, radically happy, prosperous, and fulfilled because He didn't come up with His own agenda. He discerned the invitation and made Himself available to join in with the Father even if the vision of God didn't seem popular, sensible, reasonable, or attainable.

In every generation God raises up a people who have a different spirit. The church has missed the historical context of some of the prominent people mentioned in the Bible. For example, what made Nehemiah get into the Bible? It wasn't the fact that he had a personal prophecy that he fulfilled. It was that God was building a wall around Jerusalem and Nehemiah was the one who responded to God's invitation to join Him in what He was about to do. Joshua is a historical character in the Bible, but what makes Joshua significant? It wasn't his pursuit of a personal destiny; that's how we approach it. It's that God was bringing His people into the Promised Land and had prepared somebody to lead them. Joshua was responding to the invitation of God to cross over into the Promised Land. Had Joshua failed,

God already had Caleb prepared, who was ready to do it. So, what was God doing when Moses was summoned? It wasn't his personal destiny, although you could say that had something to do with it, but the greater context is that God had decided to deliver His people out of Egypt. Do you see the trend? Was God fulfilling personal destinies over these individuals? Yes He was. However, the real story is He was addressing problems of that day and inviting willing, purposeful individuals to assist Him in solving those problems.

In Acts 13, the Apostle Paul makes reference to a time in history when the church would receive an invitation to join God in doing something that was so vast, so mind-boggling that even if it were spelled out, believers would grapple at it. The metaphor he used was the children of Israel, who because they had become so complacent, apathetic, and so timid, shrieked at the possibility of taking over territory, even though it had been promised to them. Scripture says this account of history was written so we would be reminded when we received a similar invitation (1 Corinthians 10:16). Understanding is indeed a wellspring of life (Proverbs 16:22).

In the book of Numbers, the children of Israel were going to go over into a land where seven nations were occupying their territory. When the moment of truth comes for them to proceed, they go over and find walled cities and massive structures totally occupied with intimidating systems and giant people, institutions, and voices. When they showed up and looked around, it was like looking at the Roman Coliseum and they were the sport. They said this is way too big for us; if it was empty, that's one thing, but it is actually occupied. Subsequently, they went back across the river and told their generation, it's not now and it's not for us (Numbers 13-14).

Do we understand what they did? They spied out the inheritance that God was going to give them. God knew they were too small to do it, and God knew they were too weak to do it. What they missed is that He didn't expect them to assume that **they** were able to do it. He expected them to come to the conclusion that **He** was able to do it; that "if God be for them, then who would be against them?" In other words, if God is for us, then "yes" we are able (Romans 8:31).

What, after all, was the purpose of the 40-year journey in the wilderness? Deuteronomy 8 says it was to expose to the children of Israel what was in their heart. Equally important was to train them to look at Him, not at the size of the inheritance.

But how did they respond? Two of the leaders returned with an empowering vision for their inheritance, "we are well able," but ten of the leaders returned gripped by fear with a disposition, that said, "We cannot do it." And the ten convinced the rest of the group that they could not do it. Thus our foundational scripture for this chapter, "Behold I work a work in your day . . . ;" a work that goes against the religious traditions of your forefathers and a work that you will question.

The implication for believers is God is always doing something; the key is to discern where He is at work and then join Him in "the work." And the real grid that you use to discern a personal invitation from God is to discern the activity of God in your generation and how He is inviting you to join Him in what He is about to do. Destiny and purpose are the prophetic words for this generation, and this is the real key to destiny!

We (this generation) who are kingdom people are at a crisis because history is knocking at our door and transitions are about to happen. What is the work? What is the Body of Christ missing, what invitation are we rejecting?

The world is in turmoil reaping the harvest of years of bad seed sown to include injustices, immorality, economic corruption, promiscuity and turning away from God, to name but a few. We must see what God is doing in this period of history. We must see the world through the lens of opportunity. Trauma causes people to seek answers outside of themselves. According to Matthew 24:14, during these difficult times, we are to be a witness. Luke defines what it *really* means to be a witness.

> *"And they asked him, saying, Master, but when shall these things be? and what sign will there be when these things shall come to pass? And he said, Take heed that ye be not deceived: for many shall come in my name, saying, I am Christ; and the time draweth near: go ye not therefore after them. But when ye shall hear of wars and commotions, be not terrified: for these things must first come to pass; but the end is not by and by. Then said he unto them, Nation shall rise against nation, and kingdom against kingdom: And great earthquakes shall be in divers places, and famines, and pestilences; and fearful sights and great signs shall there be from heaven. But before all these, they shall lay their hands on you, and persecute you, delivering you up to the synagogues, and into prisons, being brought before kings and rulers for my name's sake. And it shall turn to you for a testimony" (Luke 21:7-13).*

Believers are admonished not to be terrified at what's going on, because through these atrocities, God's purpose for His children will manifest. In the *New King James Version*, Luke 21:13 says, "But it will turn out for you as an occasion for testimony." In other words, these things are going to create for you an opportunity to do what you are destined to do. It will create a platform for you to step on so you can testify. Testify to what—vehemently proclaiming that "this is what the world gets for not following God?" No! Finger-pointing doesn't solve problems and frankly it infuriates the very ones whom believers are called to influence. Rather, you proclaim that not only do you have the solution to the problem, "you **are** the solution to the problem." It's recognizing your position as the one anointed to solve the problems the world is facing in every arena of living. We'll prove this point more definitively later.

Luke 21:28 says, "And when these things begin to come to pass, then look up, and lift up your heads; for your redemption draweth nigh." Let's unpack all of this. The writer is arguing that when all of these negative things begin to occur, look up. In other words, don't fall into the trap and look at the situation as the world does—doom and gloom; rather, look up, consider what God is doing, then join Him. Wow, that's powerful stuff and that's a powerful invitation.

The question is, do you see this as God setting things up for you to have an opportunity? As you read this material, you will have either a traditional viewpoint of escaping these end-time events by saying "soon and very soon, we are going to see the king," be like the ten spies and be kept contained until you die in the wilderness, or you will go to where the puck is and give

God what He wants. God wants justice. Look at how strongly he indicts the church:

> *"GOD STANDS in the assembly [of the representatives] of God; in the midst of the magistrates or judges He gives judgment [as] among the gods. How long will you [magistrates or judges] judge unjustly and show partiality to the wicked? Selah [pause, and calmly think of that]! Do justice to the weak (poor) and fatherless; maintain the rights of the afflicted and needy. Deliver the poor and needy; rescue them out of the hand of the wicked. [The magistrates and judges] know not, neither will they understand; they walk on in the darkness [of complacent satisfaction]; all the foundations of the earth [the fundamental principles upon which rests the administration of justice] are shaking. I said, You are gods [since you judge on My behalf, as My representatives]; indeed, all of you are children of the Most High. But you shall die as men and fall as one of the princes. Arise, O God, judge the earth! For to You belong all the nations" (Psalms 82: 1-8, AMP).*

He wants us to take ownership, but not in some narcissistic way surmising that we are in Goshen and none of these events will harm us. The world is looking for solutions; they are just unaware that you are the solution (until you show up as the solution). (Colossians 4:5-6).

Note: Isaiah 60:1-4:

> *"Arise, shine; for thy light is come, and the glory of the LORD is risen upon thee. For, behold, the darkness shall cover the earth, and gross darkness the people: but the LORD shall arise upon thee, and his glory shall be seen upon thee. And the Gentiles shall come to thy light, and kings to the brightness of thy rising. Lift up thine eyes round about, and see: all they gather themselves together, they come to thee: thy sons shall come from far, and thy daughters shall be nursed at thy side."*

According to this passage, they are coming to you. But why are they coming to you? They are coming because you are the solution. Note, I did not say, you have the solution, but that you are the solution. We are being repetitive on purpose. We are that generation predestined to deal with these end time pressures (Psalms 102:18, Acts 17:26, Hebrews 11:39-40).

Why is having a God-size vision so difficult for us to embrace? Our response is similar to the ten spies in Numbers 14. We spew venom at anyone trying to take us out of our eschatological comfort zone. What happened to the mentality of being the "head and not the tail, and more than a conqueror army of believers?" How did we become "in our sight and their sight like grasshoppers?" The Apostle Paul asked a similar question in Galatians 3:1, *AMP*, *"O YOU poor and silly and thoughtless and unreflecting and senseless Galatians! Who has fascinated or bewitched or cast a spell over you, unto whom—right before your very eyes—Jesus Christ (the Messiah) was openly and graphically set forth and portrayed as crucified?"* Selah!

One of the reasons we have become intimidated is due to what happened back in the 19th century when William Jennings

Bryan, a great orator and statesmen was pitted against a scientist and attorney (Darwin) who were debating over evolution in one of America's famous trials called the Scopes Monkey Trial (1925). The results of the trial affected the Christian psyche back then and I don't believe the church has ever recovered from it.

Jennings had a theology for economic empowerment and was loved and welcomed by the American and Christian culture. So, instead of the south selecting a scientist and a Christian attorney to debate against teaching evolution in the school system, they selected their favorite orator, whose great line was "I'm more interested in the *Rock of Ages* than I am in the age of rocks." Darwin clobbered him during the trial and at the end Jennings ended up looking stupid and impractical.

A whole generation of Americans observed this and Christians particularly were embarrassed because they felt they couldn't stand their own ground against science. That was the lie, the church could; it simply selected the wrong person to represent it. Unwisely, the religious community began removing themselves from educational institutions declaring Christians should "come out from among them and be separate and undefiled." This began the emergence of Christian universities and other alternative schools and Christians moving away from culture and hiding out in church. This was a defining moment in history. The religious community surrendered the best universities (Princeton, Yale, and Harvard) to the secular community. Today, these universities which incidentally were founded by evangelists for training ministers and bringing the kingdom into all sectors of society have become some of the greatest trainers of secular humanists today.

What is the intent of this segue? Our generation hasn't thought about taking dominion, except with having a Bible study at the office or a Christian in the White House. Somewhere we didn't have the strength, the Word or the revelation of who we were and what we have been sent to do. Or as suggested, perhaps the church is still recovering from the psychological blow, thinking that believers are not smart enough to rule outside of the church. Many of the five-fold ministry gifts are operating with a separatist mentality and God is saying this is not "the mentality" of my end time church. It was prophesied that the end time church would do great exploits: something of phenomenally significant and demonstrated proportions; not just little victories, but significant historical impacts (Daniel 11:32). This is the set time for the church and we will do the work (Psalms 102:13).

But we have to go where the puck is. Are you willing?

❦❦

No Grasshoppers Here

"Now what I am commanding you today is not too difficult for you or beyond your reach. It is not up in heaven, so that you have to ask, "Who will ascend into heaven to get it and proclaim it to us so we may obey it?" Nor is it beyond the sea, so that you have to ask, "Who will cross the sea to get it and proclaim it to us so we may obey it?" No, the word is very near you; it is in your mouth and in your heart so you may obey it."
Deuteronomy 30:11-14, NIV

As mentioned previously, in every generation God raises up a people who have a different spirit. When the spies went into the Promised Land, Joshua and Caleb were the only two who returned with a revelation of intimacy; that God loved them and would empower them to overcome all adversity and to reign victoriously. Their identity was more in God than in the weakness of who they were. God said, because you have a different spirit, I will use you to lead the generation into the Promised Land (Numbers 14:24) and, of course, they did (Joshua 1-4). There is always "a people" that God raises up that have an overcoming spirit to fulfill a task.

Have you heard that "small is the new big?" Well, in the Bible, David exemplifies that. David was this little guy who would play his harp. All of his brothers looked stronger than him, but he found an intimacy with God while shepherding those sheep, one in which God would back and endorse. When looking at Goliath, listen to how he talked to the men who stood by him in 1 Samuel 17:26: "For who is this uncircumcised Philistine that should defy the armies of the living God?" There has to be a mentality that rises up within the church where we defy the Goliaths that are standing in the face of the world today; Goliaths like depression, suicide, poverty, homelessness, human trafficking, injustice, etc. And they're saying "what are you going to do about it?" What we are going to do about it is exactly heaven's agenda for the end-time church.

> *"After that thou shalt come to the hill of God, where is the garrison of the Philistines: and it shall come to pass, when thou art come thither to the city, that thou shalt meet a company of prophets coming down from the high place with a psaltery, and a tabret, and a pipe, and a harp, before them; and they shall prophesy" (1 Samuel 10:5).*

What we are about to reveal is mind-blowing, but will make the end-time mandate for the church crystal clear. In 1 Samuel 9:16, God decides to anoint a king to deal with a current issue, "that he may save my people out of the hand of the Philistines: for I have looked upon my people, because their cry is come unto me." So Samuel the prophet follows the Lord's instructions to anoint Saul as king. Samuel confronts Saul and tells him to go "to the hill of God, where is the garrison of the Philistines" (1 Samuel 10:5). Here is the amazing point you MUST get. Until this moment, the connection here has been missed; this is God's hill with a demonic fortress on top of it. Why does the prophet send this man to the hill of God? So he can have his eyes opened to the fact that something is terribly wrong; there is a garrison of Philistines on **God's** hill. An equally mind-blowing point that we must point out here is the apathy towards knowing that Satan was occupying something that belonged to God and it was acceptable. Selah!

> *"Wisdom hath builded her house, she hath hewn out*
> *her seven pillars . . ." (Proverbs 9:1).*

Here the writer reveals that a house is supported by seven pillars. The metaphor is used to illustrate that there are seven structures (pillars or spheres) that all nations possess that mold that society. While we have been *having* church, Satan has been working feverishly to get God out of each of these spheres (hills). You may have heard of them referred to as seven mountains, mind molders or domains. However, what we call them is insignificant; it's simply a way of putting handles on a complex subject. The bottom line is God wants this Joshua generation with a different spirit to give Him what He wants—the "hills of God."

The Word of God declares that the kingdoms of this world will become the kingdoms of our God as depicted in the following image (Revelations 11:15).

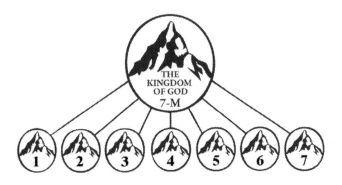

The 7 mountains are: religion, family, education, media, arts & entertainment, government, and business.

1. Religion is a mind molder and there are many religions. The church should take the mountain of religion. It should be the preeminent voice in the spiritual realm.

2. Family is a mind molder. Families are shaping their children. And if the church doesn't have a real strong dialog with the way families are running the country, then you have dysfunctional families thinking it's normal; they reject the Christian standard declaring that it is simply a religious belief.

3. Education is a mind molder. Whose ideology is shaping our children? Whoever controls the brains of our children is shaping the next generation. Hitler understood this. That's why it was mandatory for youth from age 12 to become part of the educational system that was honoring "Der Führer," the affectionate name

they called him (meaning leader or guide) and were ready to die for him.

4. Government is a mind molder because government can establish and enforce the laws, release the finances, and have the military to back it up and impose it.

5. Media: The media mountain in its own way has become the emerging great power because this is where everything is viral. Ideas are marketed from the very first moment you wake up in the morning until you recline at night. You think you are getting the truth but what you are getting is someone's version of the truth masquerading as an objective fact. He who has the power of the propaganda has the power to declare what reality really is.

6. Arts & Entertainment, the recreation in which you partake, what you are laughing at and singing with; the sports icons you celebrate, all are subconsciously programming you and shaping your opinions.

7. Business and finance is where technology and science finally come into power and this is where the finances of the world system come into play. It is a mind molder because it takes money to finance any agenda. This is also the mountain that is disciplining and influencing our children as evidenced by the clothes they wear, the music they listen to, the videos they watch and the games they play.

Some models include science and technology as a sphere, where the medical field is included, but these are the seven that shape the minds of nations. The enemy wants to occupy the top of the mountains in every one of these spheres of influence. Note in Luke 4, he boasts that all of "the kingdoms" belong to him and he can give power over these kingdoms to whomever he wills (vs. 6). He wants to get and keep God out of them so they have no value, no holiness or integrity (Proverbs 29:2). That was never supposed to happen. But the church has been one-dimensional. We go to church on Sundays and on Monday forget what manner of man we are. The Church, the most powerful entity on the planet, has been reduced to *a place* to get "my praise on," fellowship with the Lord, give my tithes and offering, hear the message and go out on Monday morning and try not to get too contaminated by being in the world.

What we are suggesting is that somehow in the course of our history as a movement in the church world, we have made a mistake; we have seen the church mountain as separate from education and government and media, arts and business, and family. The result, you have whole movements funded in order to create same-sex marriage agendas to go into school systems and teach children ideologies that will militate ultimately against the kingdom of God; government—dirty politics and media—who can believe what you read in the press, and arts, business—unclean money; having to make money, etc. The church has judged those spheres of the kingdom that have the potential to reveal Jesus and to glorify Him. Ignorantly, we separate from them in eschatology and belief systems, asserting that the whole world system is going to the antichrist anyway so why even put up an effort?

In practicality we taught that spiritual things were sacred and natural things are secular. So in this mistaken dichotomy, we have allowed a garrison of the Philistines to be constructed on the hills of God.

Through prominent evangelicals, for nearly a century, God has been trying to get this mandate to believers to influence culture (Abraham Kuyper, Francis Schaefer, Loren Cunningham and Bill Bright). Kuyper, a politician, journalist, statesman, and Pastor in Scandinavia, demonstrated this mandate throughout his country. He declared, "Each of these spheres of influence were created by God whether it be education, economic, government or arts, and has the ability to glorify God in a unique way. Every nation has its own expression and contribution." He went on to say, "There is a supernatural anointing on you to access the wisdom of God to how he designed these spheres to operate with his blessing." This, friend, occurred in 1920. How did we miss this?

We've either ignored or rejected this *transition* for the church because of a wrong worldview. The nature of a religious spirit is it wraps itself around something the Father is no longer speaking and fortifies itself against what the Father is presently doing. In other words, it hangs out where God is no longer moving.

> *"You will arise and have mercy and loving-kindness for Zion, for it is time to have pity and compassion for her; yes, the set time has come [the moment designated]"* (Psalms 102:13, AMP).

Let's be pragmatic. We have had years of preparation and training in faith from great men and women such as E.W. Kenyon, Kenneth Hagin, Oral Roberts, Kenneth & Gloria Copeland, Charles Capps, Creflo Dollar, Bill Winston, Joyce Meyer, T.D. Jakes, Marilyn Hickey, and many others. What was, after all, the purpose of this teaching? Not to mention the great "outpouring of the Holy Spirit," Who incidentally still makes His abode in believers.

According to Ephesians 4, God gave *some* to be Apostles; and *some* to be prophets; and *some* to be evangelists; and *some* to be pastors; and *some* to be teachers. If only *some* (20%) are to be in the five-fold ministry, how are the other 80% to be employed in the Kingdom of God? The five-fold ministry gifts train believers on how to release their faith to use their gifts and talents in the kingdoms of this world—these seven spheres—and how to have the character to sustain motivation. Instead we've been making more preachers. We don't need more preachers, we need more laborers. Until this message is heard and received, the other 80% will continue to be unemployed in the Kingdom of God. But there are the Joshua's and Caleb's who dare to believe; unlike most Christians who want a touch from God and to get farther away from "the world."

What is God doing right now? He is raising up a movement of saints to another level of maturity and authority in the earth where a kingdom anointing is coming upon people in those spheres to rise up and go to the top. They are not in the religion or church mountain, they are in those other six mountains.

Who has authority in the church mountain? The five-fold ministry gifts have the authority. Well, who has authority in those other spheres; those who God called into them. So if you have the call for media; script writing, movie making, the call to wealth or to medicine, which is discovery, or the call to entrepreneurial excellence, the call to be governor or mayor or judge or lawyer, that sphere belongs to you. It's the hill of God and you are the one God anointed to take out the garrison of the Philistines.

There is a champion with a company of believers that have not only been *assigned* to solve the problems in their nation, but *designed* (wired) to solve the problems in this world. Many of you are already operating in one of the seven spheres. You've just not been exposed to this revelation to know you are supposed to do more than build Pharaoh's cities, but change them.

If you are saying, "this is not our job," you are missing it and are thinking too small. This is, quite frankly, why most of the church is frustrated. The scripture says, emphatically that when vision is unknown, people run wild and because of a lack of knowledge God's people become naked—insignificant (Proverbs 29:18; Hosea 4:6). God designed you so that you operate with 100% utilization of your capacity and that is how you experience sustained revival. If you have 90% of your gifts, talents, and abilities, underutilized, you never actualize and if you never actualize, you are never fulfilled and if you are never fulfilled, you're half backslidden feeling guilty. Wow!

Oh, the power and fulfillment that awaits the believer who agrees with *heaven's agenda*. God is looking for some Daniels, Esthers, and Josephs who are willing to take assignments; to expand the boundaries of what they have so that they can give to the next generation. And heaven is waiting *to back* the serious believer who recognizes his call to solve the problems in his/her nation.

As members of the Body of Christ, believers possess what we call, "the believer's advantage and the force of favor." Favor is more than getting a close parking spot during Christmas time at the mall. It is the "irresistible Charisma of Christ that wraps itself around a believer who is fulfilling purpose that attracts everything needed to complete the assignment" (Psalms 5:12). Like a mantle, it is tangible. You can feel the thing wrap around you. It's like being dipped in honey from heaven that attracts all the resources of heaven towards you. The advantage is the ability to operate ten times better than someone in the world who is of equal competence in your sphere (Daniel 1:20).

Listen to Caleb, who as we recall had a different spirit:

> *"And now, behold, the LORD hath kept me alive, as he said, these forty and five years, even since the LORD spake this word unto Moses, while the children of Israel wandered in the wilderness: and now, lo, I am this day fourscore and five years old. As yet I am as strong this day as I was in the day that Moses sent me: as my strength was then, even so is my strength now, for war, both to go out, and to come in. Now therefore give me this mountain, whereof the LORD spake in that day; for thou heardest in that day how the Anakims were there, and that the cities were great and fenced: if so be the LORD will be with me, then I shall be able to drive them out, as the LORD said" (Joshua 14:10-12).*

You have an anointing to fix the problems on planet earth in your sphere. You are the solution to a problem in your sphere, which is why it is so ludicrous from heaven's perspective to hear

God's people on earth looking at the world getting worse and use that as an argument for why Jesus is coming back.

> *"[The purpose is] that through the church the complicated, many-sided wisdom of God in all its infinite variety and innumerable aspects might now be made known to the angelic rulers and authorities (principalities and powers) in the heavenly sphere"* (Ephesians 3:10, AMP).

We don't subscribe to a belief system that says every nation or every system is going to become Christian. We don't believe that. But we do believe that this gospel of the kingdom shall be preached in all the world as a witness and then the end shall come. We haven't preached the gospel of the kingdom, because until you go into that realm, the kingdom has not been made manifest. What we have preached is the gospel of salvation, which is a way for anyone in those realms or other areas to go to heaven when they die providing they get saved. The gospel of the kingdom is that God can do more than get you to heaven when you die. He has authority over earth right now. He is the Lord of heaven and earth. The gospel of the kingdom is the practical dominion of Christ manifested through His anointed ones administrating their sphere and assignments within these spheres. If it's broke, you fix it.

I know some of you are scratching your head in disbelief. For you we say, meditate on the scriptures in this chapter and let the Spirit of God minister to you. It is the truth. For those of you who have David's mentality, before you proceed, there's some unfinished business we must first resolve.

The New Testament validates that the kings of this world are occupying positions Satan has promoted them into and they're not chomping at the bit to give you control (Luke 4). So, there is a strongman occupying the territory that you are about to dispossess. Matthew 12:29 says, *"Or else how can one enter into a strong man's house, and spoil his goods, except he first bind the strong man? and then he will spoil his house."* That means you will have to fight the power that is occupying the house that God is calling you to possess. And the demon that you are about to displace has the authority to test you to see if you are qualified to remove it. Jesus called Satan an evil genius and declared he (Satan) had nothing (no claims) on Him. John 14:30, *Amplified,* says it this way, "[He has nothing in common with Me; there is nothing in Me that belongs to him, and he has no power over Me]."

So, "Not so fast" believers. Before you take any mountain, you must first take your mountain; you must master yourself.

❧ ❧

Not So Fast

*"And the devil, taking him up into an high
mountain, shewed unto him all the kingdoms of
the world in a moment of time. And the devil said
unto him, All this power will I give thee, and the
glory of them: for that is delivered unto me; and to
whomsoever I will I give it. If thou therefore wilt
worship me, all shall be thine. And Jesus answered
and said unto him, Get thee behind me, Satan: for it
is written, Thou shalt worship the Lord thy God, and
him only shalt thou serve." Luke 4:5-8*

Ripped from the headlines: "Pastor offered to step down after he admitted having a threesome with his wife and a male church assistant and said the encounters sometimes took place during Thursday Bible study meetings and Sundays after church; A husband and wife pastoral team is getting divorced after the husband admitted a year-long adulterous affair with a stripper; The Pastor of a mega church, married some 20 years, recently revealed to his congregation that he is gay; preacher suffering with depression attempts to kill herself with a .357 Magnum . . ."

And *we are* the generation who will defy Goliath, to manifest as sons of God in the cultures of society? Yes, we are, but these individuals and many others in the Body of Christ have not done their personal homework. They have not dealt with their issues of life. Going to church or preaching the gospel does not make you a "son" of God, just as going to McDonald's doesn't make you a hamburger. There is a process required.

I think we totally miss what Jesus is saying in Matthew 25:1-11, the parable of the ten virgins. What's the significance of the oil? We have developed an unconscious empathy and tolerance for sin. We wonder how we miss it and how "the man of God falls." You see preachers sell the oil which is what Jesus was talking about with the virgins, "Go and buy oil." This should be an 'aha' moment when you really think about it. The metaphor is those foolish virgins had to go to the people that had the oil that weren't going to meet the bridegroom themselves. Understand that it wasn't like they were onboard the plane saying, "I'm not going to need much of this; here you can have half for fifty cents." They (the preachers—the ones with the oil) weren't on the plane! Metaphorically, those virgins went back to the vendor (preachers) and the vendors were still selling, but they weren't going. In other words, the preachers were the distribution center for the anointing and revelation. That doesn't mean that they themselves were partaking of what they were carrying. That's why people look at men of God who failed and are amazed. Well, the grace, anointing and gift of God flows through the Head, Jesus, then to His five-fold ministry gifts and then to the Body of Christ. A man of God must understand the vital role he plays in the life of a believer. He must remain full of the oil and protect what God has entrusted to him. Otherwise this generation will not be equipped to defy the Goliaths of this age nor the enemy who is waiting to assail them.

That's why it matters where you go to church and who you sit under. If all the man or woman of God can do is "preach," and there is no evidence of the rulership of Christ in their lives and consequently not yours, then it's time to go where the puck is.

The parable of the virgin is clearly revealing that you have to go buy for yourself. What does the buying mean? You have to do transactions; meaning you have to invest your time, your heart, your head and your money into getting the Word, going to the right church, getting the right information, no matter the cost, so the road map will be both available and clear.

Why is this important? Because if you are not entirely healthy on the inside, while you are attempting to fulfill your assignments leading to your destiny, what you didn't master in your personal life starts to show up. This isn't hard to understand because this is the same story we often see exposed in the public lives of entertainers who end up with drug and alcohol problems, broken marriages, and who sometimes commit suicide, all because the devil is merciless in exploiting any angle given to him—in saint or sinner alike. He is an equal opportunity employer when it comes to dispensing misery.

So if you climb up that mountain of influence and you don't have your interior self—your soul—in alignment, that is the area that is going to get assailed by the enemy.

Ephesians 2:2-3, *Amplified*, says before we received Christ, we were being trained by Satan to be self-centered, impulsive, compulsive, animalistic, fleshy, and demonical people. Those characteristics don't just go away because you attend church every time the doors are opened. God is serious about dealing with these issues because He knows that the spirit that is controlling the next level of your destiny will try to keep you from rising up to it by getting you to trip up into sin patterns at the level you are at right now.

Jesus was a product of the workmanship of God's Hand and "the Body" must follow the same process. While in the wilderness, Jesus doesn't bow or take the knee. We can't miss this. He literally reveals to us how to ascend the mountain of God and never be assailed by the enemy, and it's this, "before wilderness comes workmanship" (Ephesians 2:10). Let me repeat John 14:30, *Amplified* version. Jesus says, "I will not talk with you much more, for the prince (evil genius, ruler) of the world is coming. And he has no claim on Me. [He has nothing in common with Me; there is nothing in Me that belongs to him, and he has no power over Me]." That's it! If you are to occupy the high places, you must deal with the matters of your heart. The Word says that the heart knows its own bitterness. So, it is impossible for Satan to catch you off guard. He just assails what he has a right to (Proverbs 14:10, Luke 22:31).

This was another critical purpose of the faith message. It was so that the Body of Christ could learn to live independent of the pressure to bend the knee, but to serve God with a spirit of faith to complete the dominion mandate through each assignment He would give us individually. But the faith message omitted one pivotal teaching; those darn uncontrolled emotions; what to do with our feelings. We're not to deny that we have them, but we are to deal with them. Let's continue to follow the road map to, "Personal Mastery."

Taking Your Personal Mountain

"In your patience possess ye your souls." Luke 21:19

By now, certainly the faith message has been embedded in the minds of the serious believer. "We are in Him," echoes from every Word of faith pulpit; "We are kingdom citizens, made in the image and likeness of God; we are His representatives on the Earth;" and it took some time but the radical believer has even embraced that "We are in the God class" (Psalms 82:1-6).

So, with all the information we know about spiritual life and faith, why is it that we are not consistent in being in a kingdom state? In other words, why does our mood or emotional condition from moment to moment still fluctuate? Like David who in the book of Psalms sounds like a manic-depressive, sometimes he's praising God for His faithfulness, other times he's pleading with him for escape, there are times we don't know whether someone is saved or unsaved, if we observe their incongruent behavior.

We are in the *Body*, but some of God's children are the meanest, most stubborn, insecure, jealous, competitive, rebellious, and timid people in the world. Why, because we've not given much attention to the believer's disposition. We've been taught to ignore our emotions—that as people of faith, we're not moved by how we feel. This was a critical oversight of the faith era.

During the 1980's, the Church was given a great emphasis on walking by faith instead of by feeling. That teaching was appropriate at that time because there was so little understanding of what faith really was, and it was confused with other things. But we need to come full circle now and admit that the unbalanced teaching we received on faith and not on emotions have crippled us. Romans 14:17 says, "The kingdom of God is not meat and drink, but righteousness, peace and joy in the Holy Ghost." That means two thirds of the kingdom state has to do with feelings. So, rather than stopping at, "we walk by faith and not by feelings," we should have clarified this by saying, "if you're not feeling in a kingdom state (peace and joy), use your faith to access the positive feelings you're not experiencing at the moment." We can access the peace of Jesus because He left His peace with us to enjoy, and we just saw that it is an essential value or quality of the Kingdom that is available to us. However, because we ignored the negative feelings we were having from time to time, those feelings have become strongholds and areas that are not only keeping believers out of fulfilling destiny, but areas that the enemy will assail when a believer begins to ascend the mountain God has legitimately given him/her to occupy.

It's really interesting how we missed this when you consider how many scriptures in the Word deal with emotions (Proverbs 15:13, 15; Proverbs 17:22; Proverbs 18:14 and Luke 21:19, to name a few). In fact, the *Amplified* version of Luke 21:19, uses thought-provoking language:

> *"Behold! I have given you authority and power to trample upon serpents and scorpions, and [physical and **mental strength** and ability] over all the power that the enemy [possesses]; and nothing shall in any way harm you"* (Emphasis added by authors).

This is why we believe that the Spirit of God is bringing to the forefront "the believer's mind." God does more than "prove one's work." He pays much attention to one's emotional stability, a vital key to personal mastery. Psalms 7:9, *Amplified* says, *"Oh, let the wickedness of the wicked come to an end, but establish the [uncompromisingly] righteous [those upright and in harmony with You]; for You, Who try the hearts and emotions and thinking powers, are a righteous God."* If your emotions are unstable, then your revelation carries no weight because the fruit of the spirit is not present. Where the "spirit of the Lord is," there is liberty (emancipation from bondage) [2 Corinthians 3:17]. Believers are not known by their revelation, they are known by their fruit (James 1:9; Matthew 12:13).

Notice, our Savior understood the importance of having a strong mind and temperate emotions. In 3 John 2-3, the Apostle writes, *"Dear friend, I pray that you may enjoy good health and that all may go well with you, even as your soul is getting along well"* (*NIV*). He is correlating your wholeness with prosperity of your soul (mind, will, and emotions). The soul, the seat of your emotions must be confronted. After years of neglect, we must deal with it now.

One of most disappointing handicaps we have in the Body of Christ is how we treat secular information. When you think about it, it's really ridiculous. For example, although we know nothing about the religious convictions of Thomas Edison, we use electricity unconsciously. The thought of living by candles, because "Edison may not have been a believer," is ludicrous.

If you listen very closely, you will discover that the world is using principles that actually belong to the realm of faith. While they may leave out whole segments that belong to believers or call it something else, we are not necessarily grabbing it for fear of being contaminated. It reminds me of Acts 7:57, when Stephen gives an anointed sermon, the people "cried out with a loud voice, and stopped their ears." They didn't want to listen for fear of being convinced he was right.

Let's now delve into an amazing body of information that we have discovered that has significantly enhanced our lives. It is *Emotional Intelligence*, or its shorthand name, "EQ." You are more familiar with the term IQ. Most people detest IQ tests because the scores rarely reveal one's accurate abilities, intellectual capabilities, or work ethic. They are simply tests. How many of you because of lower IQ scores felt ashamed thinking you were not intelligent enough to pursue certain career fields? And perhaps for years you avoided that career path for fear of failure; all because of a "stupid" test. Yet, for years, one's IQ was the most widely accepted predictor of life success. In determining IQ, those people with higher scores were predicted to succeed in life landing the higher paying jobs while those with lower IQs were predicted to end up in menial jobs. Consequently, many job selections were based solely on these scores. What an error!

History has unmasked mass murderers, child molesters, and corrupt corporate executives who displayed near genius IQ scores. For example, serial killers Ted Bundy, who killed 28 women, and Jeffrey Dahmer, who after killing his victims, often ate their flesh, shared very superior IQ scores (124, 121 respectively) as did Charles Manson whose hideous stare after nearly 40 years still pierces the heart, (scored 121), and Ted Kaczynski, the Unabomber scored 160-170 on the IQ test, classifying him as genius. Perhaps a less known perpetrator, Steven Russell, a U.S.

con artist and imposter, who not only defrauded many corporate executives out of money, escaped from prison so many times he was compared to Houdini. His IQ has been recorded as 163; genius.

That's why an increasing number of psychologists agree that EQ can trump IQ. It's because these examples alone demonstrate that people with high IQs can be stunningly poor pilots of their private lives. The problem is most people are oblivious to what they are thinking, feeling, or saying and how this influences their behavior. An inability to notice your true feelings leaves you at the mercy of those feelings and the enemy.

This is why EQ has become so prominent. Let's begin by defining emotions. In Latin, "*E*" is translated up, out, and away; "*motions*" is self-explanatory, and it denotes movement. We know that emotions are associated with feelings, so a practical explanation of emotions is feelings on the inside that can move you in a certain direction. Its purpose is to move you in a certain direction. Intelligence is the ability to learn or understand from experience. Emotional Intelligence then, is recognizing a feeling as it is happening. This is called self-awareness and is the keystone to emotional intelligence.

Why is the information imperative for the believer? As mentioned in the book, *Depression Exposed: A Spiritual Enlightenment on a Dark Subject*, many people think that Christians are immune to depression and other destiny-robbing diseases. Yet, many Christians deal with depression daily. We can't tell you the number of people who have approached us like Nicodemus at night wanting to discuss their 'bout with depression.' It's because Christians represent a microcosm of the world we live in. When you become born again, your thinking and feelings don't automatically change, they have to be transformed.

Transformation is another word overlooked or misunderstood by believers. Transformation is not a onetime event that occurs as some magic act accompanied by the word, "abracadabra." It is an array of process events (a term you will become intimately familiar with later) that continues until evidence appears. A good example is the parable of the sower and the seed (Mark 4:28). The sower sows the seed and the seed enters into an array of changes before it becomes the final product; first the blade, then the ear, then the full corn in the ear. Once the fruit appears, the transformation process is complete. Once you have been transformed, you have now become the manufacturing center for your behavior. It's automatic!

We were never taught to master our emotions and the critical windows of opportunity for setting down emotional habits that will govern our lives occur in childhood and adolescence. We didn't learn this at home or in school. Instead we focused on getting good grades. Now, instead of getting paid for good grades, we're paying for focusing "only" on getting good grades.

Satan is counting on believers remaining the same because he realizes it's just a matter of time before they will eventually bow down to his pressures. Let's make up some time and deal with this critical subject so as you get closer to destiny, you won't bow the knee.

The following diagram will help you understand how you are wired:

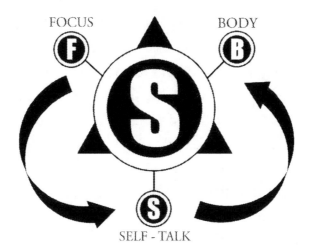

FOCUS   BODY

SELF - TALK

This triangle reveals your triad. It consists of three entities: focus, self-talk and physiology, all which run simultaneously and which in turn influences your state or internal reality (the circle in the center). When you think of **state**, think of how open or closed you are; whether you are empowered or disempowered; whether you can access the "throne of grace," and whether you are in a position to act on what you hear or feel. We will discuss this in more detail later.

Your emotional network is designed to be the by-product of whatever you are focusing on, whatever you are saying to yourself about what you're focusing on, and how your body responds to all of this mental or emotional activity. Understanding your triad will help you discern why your state fluctuates from moment to moment.

When you wake up in the morning and put a toothbrush in your mouth, you are already living in the triad, and it's already having an effect on you. Why, because it's the triad you have created. It is your triad. It is how you have trained yourself to respond to situations. You see, when something unexpected occurs in your life, for example, the sister at church says something you don't like or your spouse is not responding to you the way you want, or an unexpected calamity shows up; this "event" didn't create your state (emotional condition), it only magnified or identified the emotional patterns that you have practiced most of your life and are already living with.

Remember, "it's automatic." You are not under attack by the enemy. You are fighting what is flowing out of your own heart (belly), and it's not rivers of living water. It's rivers of constant anger, depression, anxiety, etc. You get the point? It's very important for the believer to understand whether you are under attack by a demon spirit of depression, anger, etc., or whether you are fighting something that you've practiced over the years that has become a part of your personality, or the spirit of your mind.

That means that circumstances don't make you; they simply reveal who you really are, or who you have become through years of practice. It's a triad of how you have been coping with life since the time you were a child. It's just that today when it has a face (your spouse leaving, a bad medical report, or a financial problem, for example) you think it's happening right now, but in fact you are triggering a whole series of scripts or patterns that you have developed since a child. And when you became a believer, these scripts did not automatically change.

How do these three components in your triad influence your interior state?

FOCUS is everything. Most people have no control over their focus; they are easily distracted. Whatever you focus on gets your attention and what gets your attention, gets you. What you focus on is what you are going to feel, because feelings follow focus. Your focus also determines the meaning you attach to whatever is going on in your life, which in turn determines the direction you move in. In other words, what you focus on affects what you will do. Let's use marriage as an example. If you focus on the negative things your spouse does, and that's all that has your attention, you are on a spiraling downward climb on your way to divorce court. However, if you focus on all of the qualities that attracted you to your spouse when you initially married, and give your energy to fostering the environment for that, then the honey is back on the moon (the honeymoon returns).

SELF-TALK: We all have self-talk. It's your internal dialog; the dialog you are having inside of your head or inside of yourself. It is what you say to yourself about what you are focusing on (the meaning, or interpretation you attach to what you see or focus on) and it will directly impact your state. So, if for example, your focus is on who hurt you in the church or in the past and your self-talk is, "I always get hurt; it's must be something about me," or you conclude, "I'll never let anyone close to me," then your state is going to be seriously compromised. Your ability to empower or be empowered will be nearly impossible, which is, of course, the plan of the enemy all along. Remember state is everything, because you want to be in a position, no matter what's going on around you to access heaven.

It was discovered in an emotional intelligence study that people think at a rate of 1,500 words per minute and 80% of that is at an unconscious level. Wow, 1500 wpm flow through our minds every 60 seconds and we are oblivious to 80% of those thoughts? That means there are times that you are unaware of what you are saying to yourself. This is what makes self-talk so challenging. The good news, however, is you have been wired in such a neurological way that your body will expose your self-talk.

PHYSIOLOGY: This completes the triad. It is a 10-dollar word for body. It always exposes your interior state. You see these feelings are transferred through self-talk and what gives it away is the corresponding behavior (anger, anxiety, agitation, fear, sweating, heavy breathing, lip quivering, etc.). Pain is a great indicator, because when you feel pain (emotional or physical), that means something is out of alignment. Likewise, when you are pulled over to the sideline by an emotional battle, you can process that emotion to come to a resolution. You can discern what is going on, but it starts with awareness, not denial.

"Allow me, Dr. Belinda Moss, to share a personal account of the importance of knowing your EQ. While taking my comprehensive exams for my doctoral degree, although I achieved a 3.93 GPA and had completed 30 courses, my emotional state was tested beyond measure, nearly resulting in having a nervous breakdown. Let's use the TRIAD to unveil the cause of my emotional collapse. First of all, I was the first African-American doctoral student in the program and the first military member accepted in a post-graduate degree program outside of my career-field. My focus during the exams was on not failing. My self-talk reflected fears about validating the stereotypes about inferior academic achievement for blacks in higher education, not to mention my credibility as a military officer. My internal state was so compromised that emotionally, I couldn't think and physically, I lost eight pounds the week of the exams.

Although I passed with flying colors, it was one of the most painful experiences of my life. My feelings followed my focus (failure), which was affected by my negative self-talk (disappointing others), manifesting in my body collapsing (headaches and unintentional weight loss)."

Take note of the effect of uncontrolled emotions and their effect on the human body. The effect of a chemical imbalance on the body is tied directly to the emotional state of a person. The medical field only validates what the Word of God has proven to be true (Proverbs 14:30, *AMP*).

Again, understanding is a wellspring of life for those who have it. So let's deal with the findings of this emotional intelligence study that asserts that 80% of our thoughts are at an unconscious level. We are believers and that is far too much chatter not to understand and correct.

Lights, Camera, Action

"For the Word that God speaks is alive and full
of power [making it active, operative, energizing,
and effective]; it is sharper than any two-edged
sword, penetrating to the dividing line of the
breath of life (soul) and [the immortal] spirit,
and of joints and marrow [of the deepest parts of
our nature], exposing and sifting and analyzing
and judging the very thoughts and purposes
of the heart. And not a creature exists that is
concealed from His sight, but all things are open
and exposed, naked and defenseless to the eyes of
Him with Whom we have to do."
Hebrews 4:12-13, AMP

J esus asked the disciples, "Who do men say that I am?" When
Peter responded with revelation, our Lord responded, "flesh
and blood has not revealed this to you, but my Father."
The question I have for you is, "who are you? Do you really
know who you are?" I didn't ask what you do, but who are
you? The problem is most believers do not know who they are
according to the scriptures. They have not "found themselves in
the scriptures." Even Jesus had to find Himself in the scripture
(Luke 4:18-19).

Regarding your true identity, once you find Jesus in the
scripture you can find yourself. Let's say you were lost in a

crowd of people and we were helping your father to look for you. We would be looking for someone that resembles your father because you were in your father before you were born—you have his genes therefore in many ways you look like him. This is what we call the "law of inclusion." This principle was established by God to ensure that identity would never be lost in all creation. The nature of a seed is that a seed produces after its own kind, whose seed is in itself (Genesis 1:11-12).

How does this apply here? God has chosen us **in Him** before the foundation of the world (Ephesians 1:4) and that settles any identity crisis. If you were chosen in Him, which the scripture clearly states, then the law of inclusion applies to you—in fact, it applies to everyone born of Christ Jesus. What does this really mean? It means that everything that Jesus experienced, we experienced because we were in Him when He experienced it (Romans 5:12, 6:5). He experienced victory in every arena of life. So, the question is, "Now, do you know who you are?"

Unsuspectingly, most believers come into the kingdom of God with a script that has been written from past generations, family history, scars, media, and environment. These scripts must be re-written and this doesn't occur simply by ***attending*** church.

What was happening to you when you were living a life separated from God? According to Ephesians 2, you were being *coached* by the devil. As the *director* of your life, he gave you parts (scripts) that included hurts, pains, brokenness, confusion, jealousies, pride, distrust, anger, selfishness, hardness; you name it, it's in there. These things you believed have become the script that you carry within and ultimately is the source of that unconscious disempowering chatter (or self talk).

The scripts you carry within define you to yourself. They mess with how you see yourself, others, and the world around you. These scripts are the lenses through which you view your life. Consequently those deeply embedded and disempowering scripts have a profound influence on how you are likely to behave in a given situation.

Here is a biblical example of how scripts are created and how dangerous they can become. Think about when God told Samuel to go to Jesse's house to anoint a king amongst his **sons**. Do you realize that it was Jesse (the father) who paraded his **boys** before Samuel and that he purposely omitted David (**also his son**)? I know we look at David as the young kid who loved shepherding the sheep and nothing else. But later, when none of his brothers were selected for this "promotion," he was called in. Picture what he observed: all of his brothers had already been lined up; unlike himself, they had a chance to clean themselves and look their best which incidentally their "father" ensured. David was, from his sibling's perspective, and perhaps he acquiesced, an afterthought. How did this script play out through the rest of his life? Is it possible that it contributed to why he "had to have Bathsheba?" You know like anorexia; was it a control thing? After all, he was king; he could have had any single "beautiful" woman he wanted. Listen, the devil was back there then and is always at work. You see how scripts if not re-written can return to assail you?

Infants are amazing because they start out with no scripts—they don't have dysfunctional graffiti written all over the inside of their head. We were dining out one Sunday and this vibrant little girl, about four years old, was having a blast. We smiled at her and encouraged her freedom. When her dad was ready to depart, she came over to our table and kissed us both. Although she did not share our ethnic background, she had no script that identified us as anything other than two lovely people who she was leaving behind.

That's what so beautiful about children. They are so spontaneous, vulnerable, and innocent, until they are exposed to toxic experiences in life. They must be protected from these debilitating scripts, which is why it is one of the greatest privileges in life for parents to be chosen as representatives of God to equip the next generation for their assignments in the kingdom of God.

In fact, the main script that has the most power is the script involving your childhood, often centering on relationships with your parents and other loved ones. It is the script written by an *absent* father or abusive relative. Sometimes it's the thing that should have been said by the father, but wasn't, or worse, the thing that *was* said that *shouldn't have been said.* It's the script written by a perception that a guy liked a best friend or sister better than he did the other or the dismissal of someone because of their weight or height. It's all stored in their script. Another script might be saying, "this always happens to me," or "you see, nothing works for me." It may be a script written by a teacher who never believed in his student or a sibling who seemed to get more attention than the other. What's in your script? The bottom line is your brain has a whole lot of toxic scripting and programming that it will impose on you.

Because these issues were not dealt with, they became "your" script and you've been reading and acting out your lines most of your life. Until you learn to discern what's going on and are challenged to look introspectively at who you really are or have *become* as a result of life's experiences, these scripts have the propensity to create a destructive atmosphere around you and attract people and things you don't want. As a believer, you must choose the right script to take advantage of life or life will take advantage of you, simply because you continue to choose and follow the wrong script.

One of the missing links in individuals, and that can have a dramatic impact on one's behavior and deepest scripts, is **T**otal **U**nconditional **A**cceptance (TUA). We are our own worst critics. Either we don't like the way we look, our relationship with others, or sense any significance in life. We must come to the place where we love ourselves—despite the fact that we have not achieved our optimum goal in life whether we are unemployed, underemployed, overweight, thin, married, single, rich, or poor, blahblahblah.

The way your script contextualizes your needs reveals a great deal about how you talk to yourself. You don't want to beat up yourself because that's not TUA. Anything less than TUA causes you to traumatize the part of you that is most vulnerable.

If I were to ask you to name four of your closest friends with whom you feel you can share your most intimate thoughts, I am almost assured that leading the list or probably not making the list, is you! That is because you are probably not your best friend, but rather "the accuser of the brethren." Interestingly, the four that are on your list are there undoubtedly because they give you TUA. TUA of yourself and others is essential. You must learn to appreciate your strengths and weaknesses, understanding that each plays a role in your life.

Why is TUA so important? Because you can't give away what you don't have and the Kingdom of God is based on empowering others. John 10:10 says that Jesus came that "we might have . . ." and in Isaiah 53:11, *Amplified,* we see how He was able to fulfill that assignment. The *NLT* version of that scripture says, *"And because of what he has experienced, my righteous servant will make it possible for many to be counted righteous, for he will bear all their sins."*

TUA is based on having the love of God shed abroad in your heart for God, yourself and your neighbor, that when you see injustice, you are chomping at the bit to provide the solution. You can't do that with a disempowering attitude about yourself, others or your nation.

Of course, for some, you have overcompensated. Some of you think too much of yourselves, but that too my friend is because of some script you are rehearsing due to some past experience because that is not the nature of God and God in fact hates pride (Romans 12:3; Proverbs 6:16; 1 Peter 5:5).

The bottom line is you must understand the transcript that you are working in your head and in your heart and how it is affecting the way you behave. All people have the potential for greatness, however, the limiting factor happens to be your mind, which means the degree to which you allow salvation to be worked out in the way you think, the way you speak and act, and the way you see, perceive and process reality; the maps you are working with.

You may ask, "What can we do with these thoughts and feelings that make up our script?" In other words, what do you do with your thoughts and feelings? Very simply, be aware. It is awareness, not perfection that causes growth. The moment that you have a script go off on the inside of you, and you catch it, you're able to put handles on what you're thinking and feeling.

That's where re-writing those scripts become so important. Why do you think the Apostle Paul was so adamant about reminding or admonishing believers of the necessity of renewing the mind? (See Romans 12:1-2 and Ephesians 4:23). He realized it was the only possibility for transformation. You must realize that if any addiction (anything you practice repeatedly and heed to whether physical or mental becomes an addiction) is going to be broken, it is through the renewing of the mind. My friend, all addictions whether to drugs, food, sex, scripts, etc., have withdrawal symptoms. These symptoms can manifest themselves in thoughts of fear, loneliness, depression, low self-esteem, etc. Renewing the mind empowers you to **grow** through versus **go** through time after time. If you continue to grow, transformation will be achieved.

The Apostle Paul recognized this. Acting out his toxic script nearly cost him his destiny. And oh, what a destiny! He renewed his mind with the Word of God and now we are being empowered from his transformation; he wrote two-thirds of the New Testament.

Part of renewing the mind is identifying the disempowering scripts and belief systems you have. And part of finding those scripts and beliefs is looking at the state you are in. Again, how do you know with certainty what you are thinking with 1,500 words a minute running through your head and 80% of it is unconscious? How do you know what you're thinking, especially when in the crush of daily activity and pressure you're not even conscious, you're just on automatic pilot? State is everything and awareness is a gift.

The second chapter of Ephesians reveals a powerful prosperity message for the believer. We were once estranged from God, being trained by the enemy, but now, *"you are no longer outsiders (exiles, migrants, and aliens, excluded from the rights of citizens), but you now share citizenship with the saints (God's own people, consecrated and set apart for Himself); and you belong to God's [own] household"* (Ephesians 2:19, *AMP*).

What happens now is we are being trained by God (even as you read this book). We are not only developing a new script, but we have a new Director. How does God work with us to rewrite those disempowering scripts? Enter the mysterious and exciting world of "Process Events."

The Shaping of a Champion

*"Be assured and understand that the trial and
proving of your faith bring out endurance and
steadfastness and patience. But let endurance and
steadfastness and patience have full play and do a
thorough work, so that you may be [people] perfectly
and fully developed [with no defects], lacking in
nothing." James 1:3-4, AMP*

You must understand that in your life you are going to experience challenges and that doesn't mean that something is wrong with you. Jesus told the disciples at the last supper that they had been with Him during "all of His trials and temptations." The truth is He wasn't doing anything wrong. He was doing something right and it produced trials. His feat at Gethsemane was not because of something He did wrong. It was what He had been preparing for all of His life. It was the mature level of growth in His life that made Him the author of salvation. It was His completed experience that brought Him to a state of perfection. There were many events in His life where He learned how to obey the will of the Father despite the pressure of the trial. He practiced what he learned from previous events until He was made perfect. He matured through various applications of labor, growth, and development in mental and moral character. In other words, He learned to manage His state of being and achieve victory regardless of what He faced

(Hebrews 5:8-9). There's a saying that "practice makes perfect," but what it really means is you will mature in what you practice whether it's good or bad, e.g., sin when it is fully matured, brings forth death (James 1:15).

Where are we going with this? God has a way of ensuring that you are in a position to be promoted to the next level of assignment and not proceed too quickly into an area that you are not ready for and that is through "Process Events." Consider King David. Goliath opened up the door for David's promotion into getting married into the king's family; he is now the king's son-in-law. Things are beginning to look very good for David, but that is the moment when God shifts; enter Process Events.

Process Events occur when God uses circumstances in order to get at a development phase in your life to move you from where you are to the next level. It's what you invoke intercessors to go to warfare over. Because you are convinced it is not God. Process Events can be short or long depending on their nature and how you respond to them. They are typically areas in your life that are going to stretch you and inconvenience you; areas that you will perceive as the enemy. This is important because if you are really smart, you will be able to know that where you are ultimately going isn't measured by where you are right now, or even the next invitation, but that if you see the process, you will know God has you in preparation for your ultimate destiny.

The main point you are to catch is that Process Events are a part of life. But let's not get it twisted; we are not speaking of problems you generate because of sin patterns, disobedience, or wrong decisions; or God putting some kind of sickness on you or calamity in your life. They are events that occur in your life that God can use to perfect you.

And here is the process: many of you love to receive prophetic impartation or an anointed word to manifest destiny in your life. That's why we have people seeking personal prophecies or someone to lay hands on them. We all want to hear a prophetic word to bask in the presence of the Lord. That's what we want. But the reason we have so many people with a journal of personal and corporate prophetic words, revelations, visitations, a library of books and CD's, etc., and no manifestations is because they don't understand the process. What's the process? It's what happens *between* the moments of impartation, prophecy and visitation that bring us to maturity. Very little fruit grows on the top of the mountains. It all grows in the lush valley.

While conducting a Personal Mastery Seminar for the United States Military, at the end of the presentation one of the participants was amazed at this revelation. Born in the Caribbean, he said he often looked at the mountains and then the valleys and noticed that it was in the valley that things would grow. It was an "aha moment" for him.

Note 1 Timothy 4:8, *AMP*:

> *"For physical training is of some value (useful for a little), but godliness (spiritual training) is useful and of value in everything and in every way, for it holds promise for the present life and also for the life which is to come."*

Because we are physical fitness enthusiasts, we can use this scripture to help you understand Process Events. For weight management, it is imperative to incorporate strength training into your workout. The key is, resistance builds muscle, and muscle burns fat. It gives you that glorious body most people dream of, but are unwillingly to work for. You know what happens when you're lifting and you feel that burn? That's called lactic acid and no body fat can survive in that environment. The body begins to transform and become lean.

Likewise, during the Process Events, you are becoming lean in how you think, and because you are building mental toughness, you begin to lose the heaviness (fat) that was connected to your old script. Proverbs 12:25 says, *"Heaviness in the heart of man maketh it stoop: but a good word maketh it glad."*

James confirms that Process Events are the way that God matures us (James 1:12). What is it that you're really learning when you're going through a Process Event? The script that God is after in you is manifesting before your very eyes as He disciplines and teaches you how to walk in the script that **He** predestined for you—that's it.

Remember what God said to the children of Israel when they came out of the wilderness? He said, *"I humbled you to prove you, to test you, to show you that man doesn't live by bread alone but by every word that proceeds out of the mouth of God"* (Deuteronomy 8:1-14). What was He saying? "I was testing you there to let the weaknesses come up in you to teach you how to choose the right choices and identify the consequences of bad choices." He was disciplining; "as a Father disciplines His sons, so does the Lord discipline you because He loves you" (2 Timothy 3:16, Hebrews 12:6-12).

What does this tell you? It tells you that most of your Process Events are God trying to teach you principles that you still don't have; some values you need to reinforce. When you get the lesson, your script begins to change. So, if you want to get to your place of destiny faster, your focus should be to try to discover what is the value or principle that God is working on right now? Typically there is one issue at a time, not a dozen.

To make this practical, let's go back and use the *triad* we've become familiar with to work through a Process Event. Instead of focusing on how bad it seems or what in the world is going on, or why do bad things happen to good people, instead you ask, "what is the principle that I need to be seeking first that aligns with the kingdom so that I can walk in an overcoming state. Where do I renew my mind?" That's why state awareness is so important.

When you're in trouble, have a problem, enter a test or Process Event, the number one thing you need is wisdom. Do you know what that means? It means that you need a bigger picture. Why, because you don't really know what's going on. You just think you know. Everyone has a story. You will rehearse why you are at this place, where this place is and what you need, but you don't really know what's going on. You need wisdom because wisdom reframes the questions you should be asking. For example, "why do people always do this to me?" is the wrong question! Wisdom is the ability to have a true perspective on your Process Events.

But here is the key idea, if anyone lacks wisdom, when he's going through a process or challenge, let him ask of God. Why do you want to ask for wisdom when you are going through a trial? You'd probably rather ask for power to overcome it, deliverance from it or a change in the situation. God says no, pray for wisdom. You know why you are to pray that way? Because wisdom is the ability to divest your ego from the assumption that you know the answer and invest your ego with "leaning not to your own understanding, but to acknowledge Him in all your ways." So, you humble yourself and say, God what's happening here that I don't see; what's going on that I don't understand; what's in this cycle for my life that I can now mature in so that I don't have to spend another day, week, month, or year in the wilderness aimlessly wandering through life?

Finally, let's use the life of Joseph and David as an illustration of the purpose or effects of the challenges we often face.

Joseph had an edifying dream (mountaintop), revealed it to his brothers which caused considerable backlash. His brothers put him in a pit (valley); then he was sold to Potiphar, where he ended up managing his house (mountaintop). Then he was accused of raping his boss' wife (valley); put in jail, but while there excelled (mountaintop). He was promised vindication and release but forgotten about (valley). Then he was remembered and placed before Pharaoh where his competence in the business sphere was recognized (which incidentally he learned through all of the Process Events from the pit to the jail) and resulted in him ruling over Egypt and preserving the Jewish race. Not only was it another mountaintop experience, but destiny. His entire family came to Egypt and bowed at his feet. The dream he had was not only fulfilled, but exceeded (Ephesians 3:20).

What was Joseph learning during these Process Events? He was learning humility, integrity and perseverance; his gifts were being perfected, etc. So, we go from mountaintop down to the valley, and back up and then down again. This is the rollercoaster of your life's journey.

King David's life story revealed in the book of Psalms is another depiction of the *beauty* of Process Events. We can experience the highs and lows of his journey right along with him. In one moment he is triumphing over his enemies, and in the next he is groaning and lamenting his fate. He's up, then down, then up, then down again. It's like the journal of a musical manic-depressive. So what is David doing? You'll notice in many of his Psalms there is a moment when David readjusts his focus to see things from God's perspective. This is true of all of us. We must tap in to the wisdom of what is being handed to us during the process of transition, so we don't want to rush it or quit too soon. David started off as a little boy shepherding the sheep, a champion over Goliath, and then King.

To demonstrate this, let us use your hand to help you understand the power of Process Events and their ultimate purpose. The tips of your fingers depict: impartations, impartations, visitations, visitations, and prophecies for example (all the great things you like). In between your fingers are the process, process, process, process and more Process Events that occur (all the challenges you question and wish would disappear). But observe the result of this roller coaster ride when you successfully complete each Process Event: you receive a crown of glory like the image depicted! This was the result for both Joseph and King David.

People who don't understand Process Events can't understand why they are having so much difficulty. However, Process Events are the circumstances that shape you to become who you really are if you will cooperate with the process. Knowing this reassures you that during the process in between "peak" moments, as in David's case, there is a latter end. This is what we call the art of achievement. It is really the science of how you re-write your script and evolve into the person you were destined to be, not someone else's rendition of who you are supposed to be. So, you can get to the place where you can TRULY ENJOY THE PROCESS!

Let's use weight management again to bring this point home. Many people battle with gaining and losing weight. They fail to understand the process of events associated with living a healthy life. They love to eat, but they don't like to exercise. The script to become developed in is to love to eat the right foods and to love to exercise the body to achieve the desired results. "Desire accomplished is sweet to the soul" (Proverbs 13:19).

Lastly, assignments are important because they are God's invitations to join Him in what He is doing. So, process is merely what you don't like that is happening in this phase of the assignment. But it is beautiful how perspective empowers you because once you know you are in a process, it removes the enemy from the equation in terms of what he would love to do which is get into your head because all warfare is mind games.

You must learn to be calm when you are uncomfortable, because when you don't understand what's going on, that something is being worked in or out of you, the warfare in your mind will eventually fatigue you. And that can be costly. Not only does bailing out of the process too soon hurt others, but in David's life, for example, one of the worst episodes of his journey to the throne occurred 24 hours before his promotion. He was awarded the crown like the one pictured previously. An interesting note, however, is that the crown does not endure to every generation (Proverbs 27:24), meaning every individual must overcome their own Process Events.

Let me remind you once again that what's really happening during trials is your script is being re-written. This is powerful stuff. Whenever you rewrite one of your life long scripts, you access a whole new level of YOU. But this starts with state management and there are only two states: empowered and disempowered. Let's look at this.

꧁꧂

Enter Heaven's Zone

"And he dreamed, and behold a ladder set up on
the earth, and the top of it reached to heaven: and
behold the angels of God ascending and descending
on it." Genesis 28:12

N ow the fun begins. Let's start to connect the dots here. Why is this discussion on emotional intelligence, particularly checking in with your feelings and managing them at all times, so critical to the believer? It is because believers have something that unbelievers do not have. As a believer, you have access to the "throne of grace." The Bible says come boldly unto the throne of grace (Hebrews 4:16). As ecclesia, we have underestimated and thus, underutilized the power of grace. Yes, it is unmerited (undeserved) favor but it is so much more. Grace is supernatural or divine enablement. One version of James 4:6 describes grace as a steady current of supernatural enablement (*Amplified*) which means when you plug into the grace of God, you plug into an ability that God has given you that supernaturally flows through you so that you become able to do something in the spirit that you could never do in your own natural ability. That's the beauty of the Christian life (1 Corinthians 15:10).

Let's introduce something here called the Law of Attraction. Simply stated it is when God takes notice of you—that you have done your personal homework and now He can trust you to partake in something greater than yourself, which ultimately is your divine purpose. It's similar to favor where the irresistible charisma of Christ wraps itself around you to *attract* to you all the resources you need to fulfill your assignment. It can also be described as being dipped into heavenly honey that causes all your resources to come to you and stick to you.

So, if *attraction* has something to do with *harmonizing* with God's purposes, then it is really important that you are in a state that is receptive to God's purposes. What the enemy does is assails your heart and your mind and your emotions and your thoughts with anxiety, trouble, or strife, but let's be smart, for what purpose? He does it to block you from hitting that synchronization with heaven; that cadence that puts you into alignment with heaven's voice and God's intervention on your behalf.

We like to refer to it as hitting "the Wi-Fi zone." In the natural, Wi-Fi is short for Wireless Fidelity. It is a way to use computers anywhere there is a signal but without the messy wires. Likewise, every believer has an ability to access heaven's Wi-Fi zone as long as they remain in an empowered state.

So state is everything! You have to maintain or walk in a state that is conducive to the peace of God, the voice of God, to the wisdom of God, to the angelic intervention of God, to the favor of God, to the promotion of God, because proximity is power. Before you obtain breakthrough in promotion in the natural, you have to leverage proximity in the one place you have access to that the world cannot compete with and that is in the presence of Almighty God. No wonder Satan's motive is to keep God's people in a state of unrest—so you cannot access that place freely given to you (John 14:27).

In fulfilling His assignment on earth, notice the valuable example Jesus left for us:

> *"Then answered Jesus and said unto them, Verily, verily, I say unto you, The Son can do nothing of himself, but what he seeth the Father do: for what things soever he doeth, these also doeth the Son likewise. For the Father loveth the Son, and sheweth him all things that himself doeth: and he will shew him greater works than these, that ye may marvel" (John 5:19-20).*

He said, "What He **sees** the Father doing." Let's unpack this. One does not see with the natural eye but through the spirit of their mind. What is the "spirit" of the mind? It's how the mind has become fortified through what an individual has practiced, developed, and become matured in. It manifests itself as the personality of that person. Both heaven and hell contact us through the spirit of our minds (Ephesians 1:17-18). God's Wi-Fi is to give us the spirit of wisdom and revelation in the knowledge of Him. Satan's Wi-Fi is to blind our minds to God so that he can give us the spirit of deception (2 Corinthians 4:4).

That means your success in fulfilling the plan of God for your life depends on state management. Focus is one part of what creates the dynamic of your state and there is only two states that you can be in, empowered or a disempowered. You are either in a creative state that is resourceful or closed or constricted state that is unresourceful. More emphatically, people who are in a constricted state are often controlling and do not have the ability to recognize that being locked up (closed) is causing an agreement with darkness to exist and persist in a situation that can be resolved with more openness and creativity, or that their Wi-Fi signal is being blocked to heaven's strategies for that situation.

Realize that if the Kingdom is comprised of righteousness, peace and joy in the Holy Ghost (Romans 14:17), then two-thirds of the Kingdom's qualities (peace and joy) comprise an "altered state." If more believers accessed their "altered state," not only would there be less demand for Prozac in the church, they would access another unique capacity the world doesn't have and that is a kingdom dimension.

According to Hebrews, it is possible for a believer to access a place where one can taste "the power of the age to come." Let's read that: *"For it is impossible [to restore and bring again to repentance] those who have been once for all enlightened, who have consciously tasted the heavenly gift and have become sharers of the Holy Spirit, and have felt how good the Word of God is and the mighty powers of the age and world to come"* (Hebrews 6:4-5).

What does this mean? According to the gospel before the end comes, the gospel of the kingdom will be preached as a witness to the whole world (Matthew 24:14). What is the kingdom? It is the government of God, the rule of God, and the way God operates. An exegesis would describe the kingdom as the future rule of Christ that "invades time right now." There is a kingdom in the future of Christ's undisputed reign and Hebrews says that as a believer you "here" get to see it and "bring it into the present;" that when you bring the future kingdom into the present kingdom, you've taken the age to come and invaded the age that is demonstrating the gospel of the kingdom now. Hold on, "it is unto you to understand the mysteries of the kingdom of God" (Matthew 13:11). You can grasp this.

It really is quite simple to understand this truth. We hear so much about the supernatural. Although understanding the supernatural as God putting his super on our natural or being able to operate in a realm that is not subject to the world's system is true, this definition is also inadequate. When we enter into the supernatural, what we are really doing is tasting the power of the age to come. How so? In the kingdom of God, there is no sickness so when someone receives healing now, they have accessed what is available in the age to come and manifested it in the present. There is no demonic oppression in the age to come, so when someone is delivered now, they have accessed the power of the age to come. In the age to come there is no financial shortage, so when there is a wealth transfer, debt cancellation or resolutions to financial crisis, they have accessed it now.

Visionary people of God taste the power of the age to come. By seeing the kingdom (in the future) it gives them access to solutions to today's problems that they can bring back into this age. They have the keys to unlock the future and bring it into the present (Matthew 16:17-19). Wow!

What is the purpose after all, of the gold dust and feathers or the miracles we heard so much about in the Toronto revival or Bethel Church in Redding, California? The purpose is God is demonstrating to the people the reality that there is an age coming of which they can participate in right now. God is proving to us that *that* age is real and that it is dominated by our Lord Jesus who is doing these miracles and we have access to it; that's the gospel of the kingdom (John 14:10).

According to Matthew, in the last days, "the powers of the heavens shall be shaken" (Matthew 24:29-30). Most believers don't get this metaphor. Jesus said that when shaking, tribulation, and trouble comes, perhaps what's coming isn't the result of evil getting stronger and more powerful and more successful, maybe it's like the serpent that came out of the heat because the Apostle Paul started the fire (Acts 28). What really is this turmoil?

Luke 21:28 says, *"And when these things begin to come to pass, then look up, and lift up your heads; for your redemption draweth nigh."* A prophecy in 2009 revealed the true meaning of this verse. The prophetic word was that "both the church and the earth are in transition because heaven is getting closer to earth. A portal for the glory of God has opened for God to invade planet earth. Heaven is getting closer to earth." Matthew 24 substantiates this prophecy. It says, before Jesus comes to earth, heaven and earth are going to collide; the powers of the heavens are going to be shaken. So, why the shaking? It's because heaven is actually invading earth (redemption is drawing near). We look at all the turmoil as "Satan is so busy;" that it's the antichrist coming. It is not the antichrist coming. It is Jesus Christ coming, the antichrist manifesting.

The Apostle Paul explains that there is a *government* of hell (Ephesians 6:12). The *Amplified* version says, "For we are not wrestling with flesh and blood [contending only with physical opponents], but against the despotisms, against the powers, against [the master spirits who are] the world rulers of this present darkness, against the spirit forces of wickedness in the heavenly (supernatural) sphere." In others words, he is educating us that the government of hell is in heavenly places. You recall that he told us in 2 Corinthians 12:2, of a man (who many believe he was talking about himself) was "above fourteen years ago, (whether in the body, I cannot tell; or whether out of the body, I cannot tell: God knoweth;) such an one caught up to the **third heaven**" (emphasis added by authors). So, there are three heavens. The third heaven is where God lives and the second heaven is referring to hell's government. We don't use the nomenclature first heaven, but this is what earth is.

This is the picture we must get. Heaven is invading earth and what is happening to hell? Hell is in the middle and is getting thrust closer and closer to earth. What causes the shaking is not the devil. What's causing the shaking is God's presence. When a woman is having a baby, what causes the shaking? It is not the woman, but the baby. It is what she is carrying. When that baby is coming out, the woman may shake. She is not in control. What she is carrying is not only controlling her, but transforming her body to develop, mature, deliver and nourish what she is carrying; a child, or for this analogy, the kingdom of God within (Luke 17:21).

The kingdom is controlling the earth. Now why are nations shaking? Because everywhere that Satan has his hooks in the world systems, economies, belief systems, governments; everywhere that he has fear, greed, control, or operations and systems that are contrary to the way God wants things to happen, wherever he has a hook, it is going to manifest when he is under pressure. So everywhere in the earth that Satan has administrative control, he is manifesting (acting out) because the deliverer just walked into the deliverance room.

Here is what is happening. There is a fullness of time for Jesus to return to the earth and while He is on His way, He is literally getting closer and the kingdom is squeezing all the time. As it gets closer, the devil manifests in chaos, shaking systems; nature itself, creation is starting to shake because it is manifesting the fact that it is under siege and that the system of ownership is going from the power of darkness and the curse to the children of God. So, you see the cause behind the trauma is the invasion of the kingdom of darkness and heaven is right now invading earth and Satan is manifesting like never before because he has never been this threatened.

What's does that mean for you? It means you will have greater access to heaven than you've ever had before. Understand the peculiarity of the day you are in. Heaven is closer to you, which means you can get into the spirit, you can get into the anointing and commune with God if you have the discipline and the capacity to go there. This is what you need to know: Isaiah 60:1-4 says:

> *"Arise, shine; for thy light is come, and the glory of the LORD is risen upon thee. For, behold, the darkness shall cover the earth, and gross darkness the people: but the LORD shall arise upon thee, and his glory shall be seen upon thee. And the Gentiles shall come to thy light, and kings to the brightness of thy rising. Lift up thine eyes round about, and see: all they gather themselves together, they come to thee: thy sons shall come from far, and thy daughters shall be nursed at thy side."*

There is going to be gross darkness but the glory in you, shall be "seen on you." The translation of that is that you carry the solution to the problem that is tormenting them; you're ruling over your sphere.

Let's put this together with Hebrews 6:5, tasting the powers of the age to come. If you see the powers of the age to come, you will assess how to rule in your sphere of authority. For example in technology, you're going to reach into the millennium and grab technology that is right over there on the other side of the veil that you are called to go and you take it and come out saying, "here is what we are going to do." That my friend will make you excel above everyone else in Babylon, the world's system.

"YATEER" is the Hebrew word for excellence. The literal translation is, "the mountain or island that juts out above the rest." The testimony of the kingdom is that God is going to have people who rise up in all these spheres who do what? People who see the power of the age to come; who have a vision of the way it ought to be. Because remember, you are anointed to get the job done. You are anointed to manifest the future you perceive.

Jesus said in Mathew 10:16 that we are to be wise as serpents but harmless as doves. Therefore, the champion reserved for these last days requires two compatible characteristics; the innocence of a sheep and the militant attitude of a wolf. The harmless part we have down. But what is the disposition of the wise; it's *going into* these kingdoms and releasing the glory of God. Jesus combined these two characteristics and when you merge the two together, they create a new specie called a "Killer Sheep."

While in Israel, a preacher was asked by an elderly woman whether he knew the difference between sheep and goats. She said, "first of all, the sheep will always surrender the territory to the goats because once goats see what the sheep have, they will bully them and take possession of it. The sheep do not have a nature to want to fight. They don't have a heart for it."

That's why we surrender ground so quickly. We are like sweet pacifists. The goats also love the high places so if there is a shack, shed, or hill, they love to see and they love to be seen and will bully off any sheep because they want to be at the high place so that they can be seen and see what's going on.

As a pure sheep, you want to stay in the church mountain, a full-time job in revival and inviting the others to come to your sphere. But a killer sheep wants to go and invade territory. A killer sheep tracks with God, finds out what He is doing in his or her generation, commensurate with his particular gifting and joins Him in what He is doing.

So what we have to do is have a militant, focused, determined breed of tenacious kingdom taking, gate storming, commandos for Christ combined with a sweet, gentle, loving merciful, spirit of intercession, who are passionately devoted to Him. The believer who embraces this revelation will take on the disposition of a killer sheep. A killer sheep is Satan's worse nightmare.

The bottom line is our job is to be a testimony of the gospel of the kingdom. But you can't do that if you are constantly vacillating in a state of unrest, riddled with emotions so much that you can't see what the Father is doing.

We repeat, a killer sheep is Satan's greatest nightmare, so be prepared for the fight both before and after you answer the call; it's called frontlash and backlash. Let's prepare for it.

⍦⍦

Understanding Hell's Backlash

"Now Paul had gathered a bundle of sticks, and he
was laying them on the fire when a viper crawled out
because of the heat and fastened itself on his hand."
Acts 28:3, AMP

I n Mark 4, when Jesus was teaching on the parable of the sower, His focus was on preparing the disciples to advance the kingdom of God. In Mark 4:11-13 He asks,

"And he said unto them, Unto you it is given to know
the mystery of the kingdom of God: but unto them that
are without, all these things are done in parables: That
seeing they may see, and not perceive; and hearing
they may hear, and not understand; lest at any time
they should be converted, and their sins should be
forgiven them. And he said unto them, Know ye not this
parable? and how then will ye know all parables?"

In Mark 4:14-20, Jesus explains the parable and introduces what we call "frontlash." Frontlash contains all of the strategies that Satan uses to prevent the believer from developing a spirit of faith, without which, you will never be able to "take your mountain." This is the phase of spiritual training for the believer that produces growth, development, and ultimately transformation by the renewing of the mind. Notice that Satan's strategy focuses on "the Word." Satan comes immediately because of the Word. Why, because it contains everything that will equip the believer to fulfill God's destiny (Isaiah 61:11, *AMP*; Acts 20:32; Ephesians 1:17-23).

It is also important for you to see how much of Satan's strategy is targeted toward uncontrolled emotions. He uses such things as affliction (pressure), persecution, offense, cares of this world, deceitfulness of riches, and lusts of other things to hinder the development of Godly character. He understands that the revelation of Jesus Christ has no power without the fruit of the spirit; for as a tree is known by its fruit, so are believers known by their fruit (Matthew 12:33). Note what the Apostle Paul said about the fruit of the spirit,

> *"For ye were sometimes darkness, but now are ye light in the Lord: walk as children of light: (For the fruit of the Spirit is in all goodness and righteousness and truth;) Proving what is acceptable unto the Lord"* *(Ephesians 5:8-10).*

In Mark 4:21, we see that Satan's strategy is to keep individuals from experiencing the gift placed in them. Jesus said believers are supposed to be on a candlestick not under a bed. In Matthew 5:13-14, He makes it very clear by saying the spirit of the believer contains the "salt of the earth" and the "light of the world." Frontlash is designed to get and keep the believer under the bed so that the world will never experience the good works that was ordained by God before the foundations of the world.

Once you survive the frontlash, are allowing the Hand of God to shape you into the champion He predestined you to be from the foundation of the earth, have the favor of God wrapped around you, and are in a position to join Him in what He's doing, what you must now consider is hell's backlash. If you become preeminent in a field and become a spokesperson for the kingdom, favor will make you famous in some places you would rather not be known, and hell will give you a backlash because of the favor that you are operating in. You are going to have intercession and warfare and must be prepared for the backlash.

Jesus provides an excellent demonstration of favor backlash and how the believer is supposed to respond to it. In Mark 4, Jesus is taking the disciples into the country of the Gadarenes. His mission is to rid that area of a demonic stronghold that is acting out in a man that is terrorizing that entire region. While on the ship, on the "way to the other side," they are confronted with a storm of hurricane proportion. Jesus recognizes that this is backlash from Satan and remains calm and demonstrates what He has mastered in His spirit, "peace." The disciples, however, were very much disturbed, frantically calling on Jesus to rescue them. Jesus rebukes the storm and questions why they didn't demonstrate the same faith. The point we want you to get here is that Jesus understood the very reason the storm came; it was to prevent Him from getting to the other side, so He remained in a spirit of faith and peace and expected the same results from His disciples.

Because of ignorance and in some cases wrong teaching, believers faint in the day of adversity, uncertain whether the storms of life are from God or the devil. It is clear that this storm was from Satan because Jesus was not in the business of rebuking His Father. My friend, your faith will be tested by

Satan, but you must understand that your faith has been proven by God. This is always the focus of hell's backlash—to question what God has already proven and to get you to back off of your assignment.

Another great example of favor backlash is in Acts 28. The Apostle Paul is shipwrecked on the Island of Malta in route to Rome. While in Malta, to keep himself warm from the cold, he builds a fire. *"And when Paul had gathered a bundle of sticks, and laid them on the fire, there came a viper out of the heat, and fastened on his hand"* (verse 3). You must get this metaphor. A viper came out of the fire because of the heat. Who brought out the "heat," Paul did, because he was on his way to Rome to fulfill his assignment—to be a "witness" to Caesar and the enemy wanted to stop him.

You see, this is why the enemy comes out to attack you. He has a garrison at the top of these mountains and he is adamant about keeping those who share his ideology there. So don't be shocked that because of the heat that you bring with your anointing, you surface what is hidden and it fastens on you. That's the wrong time to go into a martyr's position saying, "Why does all this happen to me?"

If you are not discerning, you look at the natural and surmise that what's happening is God trying to teach you something. In both Jesus' and Paul's case, it wasn't God at all, it was a territorial spirit seeing an apostolic invasion and being vehement about stopping it.

"Belinda used herself as an example to explain what happens when you have no self awareness, let me use a personal situation to explain favor backlash, which we believe occurred because of the impact that we are making in the church mountain. Enter the 'A' Team.

While performing a routine procedure to check my heart rhythm, the cardiologist inadvertently ruptured my esophagus. The problem was, no one knew about the debacle until several days later when I had the most excruciating pain and swelling in my throat which ultimately landed me in the emergency room. After several radiology reports, the puncture was discovered alarming the medical staff, and resulted in an unexpected and inconvenient hospital stay.

Had I not been trained in the word of faith, their concerns and prognosis could have convinced me to receive a bad report which included the possibility of a tracheotomy. Instead, because I chose to remain calm and release my authority just as Jesus did in the storm, when they took an image of my throat the next morning, the medical staff entered my room looking perplexed with the following report: 'Somehow the tear seemed to have healed itself.' The tear my friend was gone.

You noticed I referred to the medical staff as the 'A Team.' They were an extremely well-trained and professional cardiology team, equipped to provide me quality service, which I appreciated immensely and which I told them incessantly. At no time did I allow the esophageal puncture or the prognosis to change my state. I remained in a state of empowerment and relieved the cardiologist of the visible guilt he felt due to the puncture. That's what's so important about *Personal Mastery*, you remain in a state to empower others; the role of every believer. I demonstrated such a level of Godly character; they didn't want to see me leave."

People often ask, "Why do bad things happen to good people?" The more provoking question is "what do good people do when bad things happen to them?" The answer: they stand in their authority and remain in a state of peace. When you live your life as a true believer, your growth and development will not only command heaven's attention, but also hell's attention. You become a threat to the kingdom of darkness, so your level of spiritual warfare is going to intensify. That means you can't just talk the talk, you must "prepare" the walk. You have to live your life everyday as if you were in warfare all the time (Matthew 6:33-34).

You're almost done with the instruction my friend, but we must admonish you to do the internal homework, prepare for frontlash and backlash and use one of the greatest weapons against the attacks of the enemy: know where you are at all times. In other words, take 100% responsibility for your emotional state.

❦ ❦

Take Responsibility

"And every man that striveth for the mastery is
temperate in all things. Now they do it to obtain
a corruptible crown; but we an incorruptible. I
therefore so run, not as uncertainly; so fight I, not as
one that beateth the air: But I keep under my body,
and bring it into subjection: lest that by any means,
when I have preached to others, I myself should be
a castaway." 1 Corinthians 9:25-27

The ultimate goal of this book is not to add yet another book to your collection or to create Christians with hydrocephalus heads (big heads full of information only). The goal is to bring transformation. And you my friend can change. When facing the need to change, many are "stuck," simply because they don't believe they can change or because they believe, "it's in their blood." That's why many people never lose weight, even when medically they need to. They surrender their obesity to genetics, asserting that they'll have to be overweight all their lives. But that's untrue. You can reshape your body, no matter your age or size. Likewise, you do not have to remain the same; you were not created by God that way or to remain a product of your environment; you can re-program your thinking.

The beginning of wisdom is to call things by their right names. Real mastery in any profession is the ability to make greater and finer distinctions than other people, i.e., the mastery of a brain surgeon exceeds that of a nose, ear, and eye specialist. The mastery of someone working on exotic vehicles or race cars exceeds the mechanic around the corner, etc. Mastery is measured by your ability to make better distinctions in decision making. The more vocabulary you have, the more it reflects your mastery of a subject, because distinctions are made as a result of mastery in that arena. We want you to achieve *Personal Mastery*.

As a believer, *personal mastery* is becoming skilled in the word of righteousness, your gift and your calling. It's about becoming the preeminent standard in the earth—by mastering yourself!

We've learned that the pressures in our lives reveal the programming we've been running since we were children; that simply by being born again those triads do not mysteriously or miraculously disappear. Knowledge is power and understanding is a wellspring of life. Now that you have understanding, you can begin the process of breaking the patterns of negative past programming so you can live the life that God has predestined for you. You start by accepting responsibility and becoming the pilot of your own life.

Let's start first with self-awareness. Self-awareness is a gift. Why, because once you know how you're wired, **you** can manage **you**. That's what self-awareness is. It's *personal mastery*. It's the ability to be objective about your own self; to step away from yourself and look at yourself from a third party point of view. You must discern your own internal ***state.*** Your present state is going to be your invitation to look at state management. Make a practice of checking in on your state; and use your triad (focus, self-talk, and physiology) to analyze why you are feeling what you are feeling. If you don't manage it, it will manage you. Practice catching yourself as your mind wanders; see where it's going. If your mind is wandering, follow it. If you begin to feel some discomfort, i.e., your peace is being compromised, "freeze frame" and don't ignore it. Don't allow yourself to get away with anything. At any moment, observe what your state is, stop and check in. The key is you must catch it in the moment that it is happening. Then, do the work, *"Casting down imaginations, and every high thing that exalteth itself against the knowledge of God, and bringing into captivity every thought to the obedience of Christ"* (2 Corinthians 10:5). Why do you use this strategy? Because the adversary is skilled at presenting you with a mental image of something that is not a reality. He has something to say about everything you say or do in life. This is how you defeat him—cast down the image he tries to get you to receive.

The person who knows how to manage his state speaks the truth in his heart (Psalms 15:2). What that means is he is learning how to control the scripting that is navigating his head and his emotions when something is trying to divert his focus. So if, for example, "church folk" are acting uncharacteristically around you or your spouse is being unreasonable, or your ship has not come in, and you don't learn how to control your focus and internal dialog, your mind will yield to anger, fear, or self-pity, to name a few, which sweeps you with a tremendous velocity. It happens in a nanosecond. I tell you, this is where we've missed it and the unbalanced teaching on feelings and emotions is part of the problem. Because most people are not examining what's going through their head, they get stuck in the current and live a life of facades and unfruitfulness. Yes, believers also.

By managing your state you can live in a bubble of your wise choosing because **you** can choose what **you** focus on, what **you** say to yourself and therefore choose what feelings and emotions and zone **you** are entering. That's called taking personal responsibility, the catalyst to transformation.

The first rule is that you must take 100% responsibility for the state that you are in. That means at no point can you afford the luxury of surrendering the power of the control of your state to any outside force (the economy, your spouse, your children, a family member, co-worker, global events or political developments, an irate or discourteous driver, a fellow Christian acting like an unbeliever, or clergy), nothing and no one. Why, because that's the essence of being held hostage. The moment you surrender your state **by any percentage** to an outside force, you've surrendered your personal power. Your disposition must be to take 100% responsibility for everything you're thinking, seeing, saying, feeling and doing. You refuse to surrender the option of your feelings or thinking to any force outside your control. Either you own 100% of you, or you leave a percentage open for someone else to own. Dr. Creflo Dollar, Jr. says it this way, "it doesn't matter how anyone treats you, but how you treat them." I would add, or how you respond to how they treat you. Remember, "Sticks and stones may break your bones, but words will never hurt you," unless you believe them. This is powerful stuff.

That means no matter what, you must receive or maintain a victor's not a victim's mentality. In other words, if you are wronged, falsely accused, hurt by infidelity, disrespected by your spouse or children, you take 100% responsibility for YOU. You must learn to swear to your own hurt and change not (Psalms

15:4). Your focus and self-talk cannot be "how can they do that to me," etc. You cannot have a victim's mentality, ever. Trust me, this will not only save you from hardships, it will add years worth living to your life.

The acid test for determining your emotional health or maturity is how long it takes you to get back to a resourceful state; meaning you are unshakeable on the inside. How long does it take you to go from a state of unrest—depression, anxiety, fear, heaviness, sorrow, and bitterness, into a state of peace?

Snap your fingers. That's how long it takes. You can access an empowered state in a *heartbeat* because it's a matter of flipping from one state to the next. When do you want to do that? Anytime you are not in an empowered state, you need to return back to that state.

What is it that you wait for to give you access into an empowered state? Again, this is the ultimate test of how mature you really are. It doesn't take a week of fasting, three Benny Hinn CD's, a Starbucks Macchiato, an hour of Bishop Jakes or finding an anointed church. What are you going to do if you don't have access to your CD's, Israel songs, etc., to inspire you, or your pastors to lay hands on you, and you can't soak for two hours? You have to have something on the inside that comes from the God who anoints all these props (worship music, pastors . . .).

The reality is, if the Kingdom of God is in you (Luke 17:21), you don't have to go anywhere to get there or rely on an outside source to get you there. You can access *inside* at anytime. But if you don't possess what's within, you will have to go without.

In a *heartbeat*, let's make this practical. (1) You come home from a long day and need a power nap just before dinner. You tell the kids to be quiet so you can get some rest, only to be awakened by a loud screeching voice. You jump out of bed frantically to put an end to this open defiance only to find that your child's finger got shut in the door. What is the result, instantaneous state change—in a heartbeat. All of that energy was based on a focus that was inaccurate. Once the focus changed, physiology and actions changed. (2) You receive a call from a relative who only calls when he wants something. Immediately you're uptight because you've made the decision not to bail him out again and are somewhat apprehensive about how he will respond. This time, however, he's calling to tell you of an epiphany he had the day before about your consistent display of Total Unconditional Acceptance (TUA). What is the result, instant state change—in a heartbeat. Or, (3) you're relaxing with the family after a long day and the bell rings. You think it's a salesperson. You go to the door with fire in your eyes, only to find it's the Prize Patrol from Publishers Clearing House with your million dollar check—instant state change. (Yeah, right!)

What's the point I want you to get? The moment you had information to change your focus, your state changed. This is what I want you to catch, your whole emotional state is dominated by your focus in any moment and the moment you get new information, your whole state changes automatically. The key is to work the triad. If you are not in a resourceful state, immediately let that be the opportunity to change your focus, which is your invitation to change your state. In all cases, the Word of God is your focus.

You say, yeah, Mosses, that's easier said than done. Oh no, what happens if you are in a heated argument with your spouse and your Pastor shows up unexpectedly or the phone rings and it's your Pastor—instant state change; case closed. You can access the kingdom in a heartbeat because it's a matter of flipping from one state to the next and when do you want to do that? You want to do this anytime you are not in a kingdom state. You need to return there.

That brings us to another important key element that could actually be added to the triad of transformation and that is the power of physiology in overcoming adversity.

It's no secret that having a strong spirit, soul, **and** body is crucial to being an overcomer. This is what the Apostle Paul intimated in 1 Thessalonians 5:23: *"And the very God of peace sanctify you wholly; and I pray God your **whole** spirit and soul and body be preserved blameless unto the coming of our Lord Jesus Christ"* (emphasis added by authors). He stressed the necessity of wholeness in all three parts of man. And then he literally begs the believer in Romans 12:2 to present the **body** as a living sacrifice. Of course we over-spiritualized that scripture to miss the mark on one of the important elements of the body. And that is it could be used as a weapon of warfare.

Martial artists have laid hold of this principle. They undergo a grueling physical regimen not just for self defense, but to build strength, stamina and flexibility in mind, body and spirit; designed to hone the mind, body and spirit. Likewise, for an overcoming life, your spirit (heart), soul (mind, will, and emotions) and body must work harmoniously if you are going to remain in an empowering and open state. What are we demonstrating with our bodies? Your body can become a weapon in your warfare against adversity or your body can become your adversary if you don't learn how to live a disciplined thought life.

Many are familiar with toxic goods, but what about "toxic thoughts?" Toxic thoughts can throw the body into a chemical imbalance. Proverbs 14:30 is very clear about the danger to the health of our bodies when we don't take 100% responsibility for our awareness and become a victim of uncontrolled emotions. The brain is designed to release the chemical (endocrine) to support whatever emotional signal it receives from the heart. A constant state of uncontrolled emotions affects both the mental and physical health of believers. No thought should enter into your heart without being challenged or changed to produce the emotional state that keeps you empowered at all times.

The key is to honor your body as a weapon. It is as much a part of the arsenal of your equipment in warfare as your spirit. Your body is supposed to look exactly like it is delivering the message that's on the inside of you. What you do with the body has a direct relay message with your brain in terms of your current emotional state. In other words, your body doesn't lie. Your body is so wired to your soul and spirit, that what you do physically connects with a neurological system that supports or contradicts your purpose. Your very disposition can give you victory. In other words, saying you are happy in a slouched cowering posture with no energy, is an incongruent testimony.

The implication is, if you want the triad to be on the same page victoriously, you have to take ownership of what you do with your body not only biochemically (what you eat; you can't abuse your body and expect to be an overcomer), but how you manage your physiology. While we're on this, there are too many believers who ignorantly expect the anointing to take care of their lack of discipline in their eating habits. You must get a revelation that the anointing cannot pay the tab for your poor choices, thus the increased number of believers who are dying prematurely and *full* instead of empty; i.e., never fulfilling their destiny.

Let's examine your face to explain more definitively the point that your body is a weapon of warfare. You have 80 muscles in your face and what you think, choose, and feel, wires a message to your brain as to what's going on. In other words, when you smile, it is because of the contents of the information chosen and the emotions attached to it that sends a message to your brain that says something's up. And when you frown, you send a message to your brain that says something's down. If you ask someone how they are doing, watch their entire physiology when they respond. Your physiology gives you away. It makes no sense to say you have peace and joy, etc., if the physiology in the 80 muscles in your face reflects something different. Just as in water face answers to and reflects face, so the heart of man to man (Proverbs 27:19). In other words, you can't hide your attitude.

Have you considered why people are attracted to some people and not to others? People who have mastered their physiology and emotional and internal state, attract people to them because strength is congruently being communicated to them by what they are doing. Likewise, believers who have not mastered their physiology repel most people; particularly unbelievers—the very ones they are called to attract. That means when people look at you, they ought to be able to do a scan and get an impression of what you're really like. Make sure you send a message that is congruent with whom you really are. The key is not to try to fake it so no one will know how you really feel. "To thine own self be true."

The purpose of this intention is self-awareness. Recognize what is within you (provided you have worked the processes) and that you have access to it in a *heartbeat*. Immediately assess your state and make the adjustment. Bring your body in line with your spirit because after all, a house divided will fall. Swift adjustments will yield amazing results, not only resiliency, but your destiny.

If Christ is in you (Ephesians 1:11; Colossians 1:27), then it's a question about whether you are in Christ when something happens and your emotions are assailed. The secret to remaining "In Him," is learn to bring your mind and body under the discipline of your spirit until you become unmovable and unshakable. Remember when all other kingdoms are shaking, you have a kingdom on the inside of you that is unshakable. This is how you become a city set on a hill.

No one cares about your spirituality unless they have a desperate need for something more certain than what their belief system is already delivering. When people suffer from uncertainty, they look for something they can believe in. If you are a believer, you are the solution to the world's problem. Now that you're aggressively doing the work, *personal mastery*, then the last step is to get your feet to where your face is in the future.

Feet Don't Fail Me Now

*"And the Lord said unto him, Arise, and go into the
street which is called Straight, and inquire in the
house of Judas for one called Saul, of Tarsus: for,
behold, he prayeth, And hath seen in a vision a man
named Ananias coming in, and putting his hand on
him, that he might receive his sight." Acts 9:11-12*

A s we are nearing completion of this book, let's ensure
we understand the importance of *Personal Mastery*. As
believers we are the Body of Christ, and I might add
here that our Head is known as the "Prince of *Peace;*" the state
we want to maintain (Colossians 3:15, *AMP*). What's in the head
is in the Body. Imagine what is in our head (Jesus) and therefore
in His Body. Colossians 2:9-10, *AMP*, says,

> *"For in Him the whole fullness of Deity (the Godhead)
> continues to dwell in bodily form [giving complete
> expression of the divine nature]. And you are in Him,
> made full and having come to fullness of life [in Christ
> you too are filled with the Godhead—Father, Son and
> Holy Spirit—and reach full spiritual stature]. And He
> is the Head of all rule and authority [of every angelic
> principality and power]."*

Did you hear that? I didn't ask whether you read that. I asked did you hear that? My God, that means believers have the capacity to do phenomenal exploits in these last days and the only thing stopping us is a religious spirit. Let me repeat, "The essence of a religious spirit is it wraps itself around something the Father is no longer speaking and fortifies itself against what the Father is presently doing." That's the nature of a religious spirit and why it is so dangerous. It hangs out where God is no longer moving.

Do you realize that we have a prophetic Word from the Lord Jesus Himself who said, *"I sent you to reap a crop for which you have not toiled. Other men have labored and you have stepped in to reap the results of their work"* (John 4:38, *AMP*). What does all of this mean? He is once again referring to the powers of the age to come. A great prophet shared that intercessors have already seen inventions and designs in architecture and solutions and healings; things that are in the cloud of glory that we are looking for. We have to get beyond the Pentecostal definition of stuff. The cloud is 6,000 years of the intercession of travailed warriors, the pleading of prophets and the unfinished fragments of the moves of God; mantles to be gathered. Stuff that didn't manifest in other people's lives has been stored up to be manifested in the end. That's why in John 6, Jesus said pick up all of the loaves and fishes that nothing would remain. He wasn't simply trying to teach and model efficiency. He was basically saying, "I don't want anything wasted of the supernatural that I have made available and I always give more than any revival gathered."

In these 6,000 years of intercession that has been stored up, intercessors have had visions of heaven. They have been to the library of heaven and while there they saw scrolls and books; a whole room filled with manuscripts that reveal the blueprint designs and wisdom strategies that God has for every sphere of life; designs and strategies that have not yet been opened because God's people haven't gone up yet and opened up the scrolls. One of the intercessors had a revelation of inventions and patented ideas and new technology that was prayed through with the date and the intercessor on it (e.g., 1946, 1948, 1953), that is not released to earth yet. It is already stored up waiting for the generation that will access it and bring it down.

This was also validated in Roberts Liardon's awe-inspiring book, "I Saw Heaven," where Bro. Liardon was taken up into heaven and given a tour. There he saw warehouses that stored body parts and organs, books, musical soundtracks, financial contracts, etc., waiting for God's people to tap into the spirit and take them; to make a withdrawal.

What these visionaries saw was validated by the Apostle Paul. Note Ephesians 1:3, *"Blessed be the God and Father of our Lord Jesus Christ, who hath blessed us with all spiritual blessings in heavenly places in Christ."* You must understand that the spirit realm is the parent realm. This is the kind of stuff we should live by.

That means if you haven't already done so, you must activate "the power of intention," which is simply to "will" to do the will of the Father (Proverbs 23:18; 24:14, John 4:34). You must align yourself with God, track with Him, let the favor surround you (Psalms 5:12) and then taste the power of the age to come (Hebrews 6:5). Then you will begin or continue to get glimpses of things before they happen. It's an unfolding wisdom that comes as you are adjusting your decisions because you are getting an intuition about the future and a sense of adjusting your course constantly by making adjustments in the spirit of your renewed mind.

In Acts 9, God went to Saul, showed him Ananias' face, then went back to Ananias and told him to go "where his face was." Ananias had to get up and catch up to where his face was already in the future. The moment he did, the Holy Spirit and miracles came down and Saul was healed of blindness. This is how God worked with the first born Son, Jesus Christ, as depicted in Paul's writing in 1 Corinthians 15:3, *AMP, "For I passed on to you first of all what I also had received, that Christ (the Messiah, the Anointed one) died for our sins in accordance with [what] the Scriptures [**foretold**]"* (emphasis added by authors).

Like God did with Ananias and Jesus, He has already put your face in the future. He has put you into exploits at the top of a mountain. So the challenge for the believer—each believer is to find your face in the future. Does this seem far-fetched? It shouldn't. The Apostle tells us that God knew exactly who He needed in this and any nation for the end-times; the most difficult and challenging times of our generation (Acts 17:26). This is called sovereign beginnings. God pre-determined our family of origin, parents, ethnicity, gender, birth order, physical characteristics, nationality, and timing in history. This gives new meaning and power to patriotism. Patriotism in a sense means God places you in a certain nation to serve a certain purpose to fight a certain battle at a certain point in time. It is not irrelevant. You are a citizen of two kingdoms: You are the only person that can operate in the spirit realm and at the same time be aware of your agenda and assignment for a nation.

Don't repeat the error that the children of Israel made when they were given an occupational mandate. They said, "It's not for us, it's for them" (Numbers 13). Remember this forewarning was written for our example (1 Corinthians 10:11). God knew exactly what He was doing by placing you here "at such a time as this."

Jonas Salk, the discoverer of the Polio Vaccine, said that he really didn't discover the vaccine; he was pulled inevitably towards something that was trying to reveal the vaccine to him. Bill Gates said that Microsoft software was not something that he created. He said it was a vision that he had the second year he was at Harvard and he left school for fear that if it was so clear to him, someone else must have seen the same picture. And from then on, it was a quest for him to harmonize with a future that was seeking to be made manifest.

Catch the language: purpose is a future that is seeking to be made manifest. That means you already have a place in the future.

From hence forth, like Jesus, Nehemiah, Esther, David, and Joseph, waltz with God; have a romance with Him and the invite will come allowing your feet to catch up to your face in the future. Then God will have His own champions occupying the high places. Perhaps you are not called to rule on the top of one of the mountains, but influencing the kings and decision makers who are there. This is equally as powerful. Why you? You are *designed* for it.

Wired to Excel

*"I will praise thee; for I am fearfully and wonderfully
made: marvellous are thy works; and that my soul
knoweth right well." Psalms 139:14*

One of the most prolific lies the enemy has gotten
believers to accept is the need to compete or be like
someone else. Many believers have totally ignored the
scripture that says to "compare themselves with one another, they
are without understanding and behave unwisely" (2 Corinthians
10:12, *AMP*). Like the Lord Jesus Christ, you must find yourself
in the scripture and understand what God has already made
available to you. Ephesians 1:17-19 says that God has wired each
believer to excel with the same abilities as "Christ," the Anointed
one and His anointing.

The reason that duplicating someone is such a travesty is
all people are originals, not copies. There are no two people
on the planet alike; there is no one on this earth like you. You
are unique! God orchestrated it that way. Note the wisdom
of Solomon revealed in Ecclesiastes 3:11, *AMP*, *"He has made
everything beautiful in its time. He also has planted eternity in
men's hearts and minds [a divinely implanted sense of a purpose
working through the ages which nothing under the sun but God
alone can satisfy], yet so that men cannot find out what God has
done from the beginning to the end."* This says that God placed
eternity into the blood or into the heart.

There are two words we need to unpack if we are to truly understand this scripture: *eternity* and *heart*. The literal meaning of these two words is *purpose* and *DNA* respectively. So this can be translated, "God placed purpose in man's DNA." Wow!

What do we know about DNA? For one, it contains your genetic code or blueprint. Genetics informally is the study of how parents pass on some of their characteristics to their children; DNA is inherited by children from their parents. The DNA in a person is a combination of some of the DNA from each of his or her parents. This is why children share similar traits with their parents, such as skin, hair and eye color.

This has great implications for the believer because we are in the family of God—He is our Father (Ephesians 3:15; Romans 8:15). More emphatically, another Apostle tells us that when we became born again, we were *re-gened* "*not from a mortal origin (seed, sperm), but from one that is immortal by the ever living and lasting word of God,*" (1 Peter 1:23, *AMP*). That means we carry God's DNA, the ability to operate just like Him.

But Solomon wants to convey a more existential point in his discussion on "genetics." Not only do we have the genes of our Father, God, but our very blueprint is unique. You may recall that no two individuals carry the same DNA. DNA is what gives us our uniqueness. This is so phenomenal that according to studies, "even in a blood transfusion, it is impossible that blood transfusions or marrow donations will mix with the host DNA. Cells don't readily exchange their DNA, except in the case of sexual reproduction. Even if you do have someone else's blood in your body, it is only temporary because the life span of one red blood cell is only 3-4 months. A transfusion is supposed to give someone enough blood to last until they can make their own. So while it is theoretically possible to have someone else's DNA in a sample, those cells will eventually be eliminated from the body." You know this had to be the Hand of God. Our Creator was emphatic about the originality of individuals.

You are uniquely you and God placed you on this planet with a specific gift for a specific purpose. This is what He told Jeremiah, *"Before I formed thee in the belly I knew thee; and before thou camest forth out of the womb I sanctified thee, and I ordained thee a prophet unto the nations,"* (Jeremiah 1:5). In other words, God told Jeremiah that He had called and *designed* him to do what he would do before he was even born; that before Jeremiah was born God called him to be a prophet and spoke that word into his DNA. Everything that was driving Jeremiah all of his life was what God spoke before he was born. This is powerful stuff.

There is a voice of God in your DNA. Your assignment or destiny is imprinted already in your DNA. You wonder about the images you have; an imagination starts with image, its logos (logismos); it starts with a word. Before you were born, God already *designed* you to become something huge and that word is in your DNA.

The problem, your genetic code can be altered by information that is given to your RNA (molecules involved in the transmission of DNA information). The enemy knows this and this is what he has been after from the beginning of time; to alter your information by feeding you lies.

Note Genesis 3:13, *"And the Lord God said unto the woman, what is this that thou hast done? And the woman said, the serpent beguiled me, and I did eat."* What is it that the enemy attacks? He tries to feed you information that will affect your future, this is what he did when he came into the garden and spoke to Eve. We think about the apple and the tree; it wasn't a piece of fruit, an apple. The next time you are in the shopping mall, stop by an Apple computer store. Note the Apple logo. It is a piece of the apple broken off. It speaks of information. There was a certain amount of information that God didn't want them to have at that time. They received it before their time. And the information was incorrect. So their future was attacked.

You see, the enemy is more concerned about what you reproduce in the future. He is more concerned about your future than anything else. He attacked Adam and Eve so that they would reproduce in a way that would be more damaging for the whole world and the whole earth. And that is what he does to YOU. The information he has altered in believers has left the church disillusioned, naked (Hosea 4:6, Proverbs 29:18) and basically unproductive (by God's standards anyway). For the believer to prove God's will (DNA), we must renew the mind (Romans 12:2) otherwise we will continue to live out the altered state of Adam's rebellion versus Christ's redemption.

Psalms 139:14, tells you that you are wired to excel. Again, this is the Hebrew Word "YATEER," meaning that which juts out above the rest. As a believer, you are already *hard wired* to manifest something extraordinary in this universe.

Let's discuss neuroscience for a minute. Neuroscientists study the way the brain works and are often called people readers. They could look at an individual, watch their behavior, ask a few questions, and by doing so, could read the person's personality grid. This science is so precise that sports psychologists using this discipline was able to spot talent and predict success rates so accurately that professional basketball and football teams hired them to select and analyze their players. One sports psychologist was so good, he picked out Tiger Woods when he was six years old and Michael Jordan when he was also very young. These two athletes didn't hire the sports psychologist because they already knew they were good so they didn't need anyone coaching them. But the point is he knew who they were before anyone else did. This has become a multimillion dollar profession.

Neuroscientists have discovered that there are 16 basic quadrants; four separate operating centers in the brain and in each center there are four types of personality wiring. That means there are a total of 16 maps that exist for people and every one of those maps neurologically is going to be predictable in terms of the way people think and act. The implication is *everybody* has the ability to operate at a genius level if they could fully align with the 1/16th pattern that they have. This is why you may hear terms like "she solves problems so quickly because that's how she's wired." You are wired a specific way for a specific reason—destiny.

The problem is with the way that educators measure your intelligence and we've already exposed the fallacies in the IQ test as a predictor of success. You and I were not told that we were that intelligent because if you couldn't spell *superfragilisticexpialidocious* or regurgitate all the U.S. capitols, or name all the U.S. presidents, then you weren't as bright as your classmate or co-worker, leaving you feeling intimidated. Yet that's only one type of intelligence, called rote intelligence.

Imagine what you could do if you could dial in with greater specificity on the wiring that God gave you to excel. We should be working with the wiring of our gifting so that we are maximizing our genius capacity in doing what we are designed to do rather than exhausting ourselves trying to do what somebody else gave us a job description for and told us what we have to do. Because when you are doing what you are wired to do, it is effortless and fulfilling.

And that my friend is why we have so much frustration and lawlessness in the church. I liken this to the Japanese Oranda fish. In its natural environment, it has the capacity to grow to nearly a foot. However, put it in a 2 ½ inch tank and guess what? It will grow to about 2 ½ inches. What determines how big it grows? The fish will grow to the size tank you put it in.

Likewise, you will grow to the size revelation you swim in. The reason why the church needs revival or "a great awakening," in many ways, is because it is bored and bored because it is not stimulated, it is not stimulated because it is not activated and it is not activated because it hasn't been invited to a larger tank. Thus, we are constantly swimming around the tank of the local church agenda or mission and missing the invitation to take over in our sphere of authority. That is also why YOU may be bored. You are swimming around in a tank while the ocean is beckoning you. Selah!

Most believers *and* five-fold ministry gifts don't understand that ALL work is sacred. In God's mind, work is not the way that you make a living. Adam had a job before he fell. His job was to till the garden and he worked like Edward Scissor-hands. It was sweat less; everything he touched prospered. This is what is awaiting you. You are created to be a gift. You are not here on the planet just for yourself. Every gift is designed to meet a need. You are here to meet an important need and it doesn't have to be in the church mountain. Remember He gave *some* to be apostles, *some* to be prophets, and *some* to be evangelists, and *some* to be pastors, and *some* to be teachers. That means that there are *many* who are not called to the "ministry gifts." This fact that everyone is not called into the five-fold ministry must be embraced. ALL work is sacred and we're being redundant on purpose. Let the revelation in this book give you permission to follow your dream in one of the other spheres of influence. It's what you have been *pre-wired* for and quite frankly it's where the anointing and favor exists.

We'll discuss this next point because we hear your heart as we've heard so many others who say; "but I don't know my gift." Yes you do, you simply may be ignoring it.

What you have to realize is that there were one million sperm in a race to fertilize an egg, and you won the race in the one million person marathon. (You, my friend, are one in a million). Then during the first 90 days in the womb, 100 billion neurons and brain cells begin to form. During the next 120 days, those 100 billion brain cells begin to explode. Those little neurons begin to want to connect with each other; they don't have those connection points yet, because what happens is a synapse pushes out like a little sprout and connects with another neuron and there are sparks going on between them. Now you have 100 billion cells of capacity starting to link up. By the time you are three years of age, those 100 billion cells, each one of them forming 15,000 stems and creating synapses, are firing all over the place. However, because of the fall of man, this creature formed in perfection and designed never to die, with an ability to do 100 billion times 15,000 functions, is limited to rely upon something else. Somewhere between your 10th and 14th birthday, nature wipes out half of your neurological network. But, don't get discouraged. What happens is nature starts to eliminate all the connections that are not necessary to your destiny. What stays or survives that vast neurological meltdown are your signature strengths.

When you think of "signature" strengths, think of, Ruth Chris' signature sweet potato casserole. It's unique to that particular restaurant. But in reality, a signature dish is a recipe that identifies an individual chef. When you tap into these signature strengths, you get the gift mix that makes you unique in the Body of Christ. Your signature strength is your core talent or ability that if you would wrap training around it, would cause you to excel and be 10 times better than anyone else, because no one else is like you (Daniel 1:20).

It's a sad fact that most people were not celebrated or affirmed appropriately while they were growing up for the strengths that they have, so they never grew up getting the affirmation or energy they needed in their strengths. Consequently, your core signature strengths possibly could be missed—you might not even know what they are.

At least 4-6 core strengths are inside of you. If you experiment with life, you will find that there are some things that you do with accuracy and ease that other people have difficulty with. The reason your gifts may be masked is when you are doing it, it seems easy to do. For example, if you are a communicator, you may think it's easy to talk and if you are a thinker, you say it just comes to you. Well, you must realize that not everybody can spontaneously come up with something with substance to say and say it well. This is a combination of gifts that may take you years to realize that this is unique to you.

Why is it important for you to recognize your signature strengths? Because signature strength is something that is unique to you; it is a talent that is within you that when brought to some level of skill development, it becomes a tool in the Hand of God to catapult you to destiny. Your gifts (talents and signature strengths) always connect you to your purpose. When you discover what they are by practice and by feedback from other people who see what you do well, the more you are going to discover what the purpose is that you are called to serve.

If you look carefully, you can recognize them. Watching children can help us understand others and ourselves better. Children know what they love and love what they are designed to do. They will, in a free environment of creativity, play out their God-given gifts. I heard about a little girl who at the age of about three, stopped her dad as he was leaving for work admonishing him that what he was wearing didn't match, and thus began a morning routine that would last for years of picking out his clothes. She was that good. Her sense of color, fashion, and flare was all there at the age of three! And now she is a fashion designer. Another individual, now the scheduler for a nation's cabinet minister, as a child would create a make believe desk complete with phone, agenda, and calculator and proceed to make fantasy airline reservations. Children, created in the image of God, know they are gifted and they love what they are created to do.

And we really need to get a hold of this not only for ourselves, but before we start writing graffiti on the minds of our children trying to make them what we want them to be instead of assisting them in becoming what their design demands. The *Amplified* version of Proverbs 22:6 says, "*Train up a child in the way he should go [**and in keeping with his individual gift or bent**], and when he is old he will not depart from it*" (emphasis added by authors). If we don't get revelation of this scripture, we will continue to lose the next generation.

And while we're on this, where is the future for the next generation? Over half of the people who are now in their 40's and 50's received Jesus by the time they were 20 years old. Now the statistics say that less than 4% are responding to Jesus in this same age group. Unlike many who say we are losing this generation because of the hardening of their hearts or the defilement of their minds due to MTV or BET, I surmise that's not it at all. Rather, it is because we have not presented a worldview of any substance to them.

The only reason we are penetrating only 4% of the next generation is because if we don't give them a distinct sound, they don't hear a distinct sound; one that resonates with their passion and calling; which recall it is inherent (Ecclesiastes 3:11, *AMP*). First Corinthians 14:8 says, *"For if the trumpet gives an uncertain sound, who shall prepare himself to the battle?"* We're not giving the proclamation of the kingdom.

Our children may be going to colleges, but they are discouraged, bored, disengaged with Christianity and not alive in their career. Why? Until they hear a proclamation of the kingdom, they don't realize how relevant their assignment is to advancing something substantial. They may not want, or better yet may not be called to be an evangelist or missionary, but television producers and computer software gurus. All of which can bring glory to God. Because, remember, "ALL WORK IS SACRED."

Now back to you. Let's look at Psalms 37:4, *"Delight thyself also in the LORD; and he shall give thee the desires of thine heart."* The origin of *"De"* is Latin, meaning "of the"; *"sire"* means father. So desire can be translated, "of the Father. This means that if you are communing with God, if you are walking with God, if you are praying, if you are in the Holy Spirit, in an atmosphere where **the Spirit of God really has access to you**, the desire of your heart, is of the Father.

Let's go back to the story of when Saul was anointed king as told in 1Samuel 9:19-20:

> *"And Samuel answered Saul, and said, I am the seer: go up before me unto the high place; for ye shall eat with me today, and tomorrow I will let thee go, and will tell thee all that is in thine heart. And as for thine asses that were lost three days ago, set not thy mind on them; for they are found. And on whom is all the desire of Israel? Is it not on thee, and on all thy father's house?"*

Note, the scripture says Samuel told Saul that he would tell him "all that is in your heart." What was on his **mind** was missing donkeys. What was in his **heart** was the call to a function in the kingdom. Then Samuel says, "don't worry about the donkeys they have already been found."

So, the issue with you my friend isn't the donkeys, it's what is in your heart. What was in Saul's heart; his true identity as a king. But it was not a cultivated revelation yet. So in a sense, the revelation you are receiving as you read this is to help you connect to what is in your heart already. Which is why every time we preach this message on destiny, it causes an instantaneous gush of feelings and tears because it's not like it's the first time you ever heard it; it's like a validation of something very sacred, very secret of something you haven't said for fear that other people might ridicule you if they heard it.

For some of you, this prophetic word will be speaking to what's in your heart, but guess what? Your head may not be in agreement to what's in your heart. Because your history is in your head and your destiny is in your heart.

So the dream you have, the vision you have, the re-occurring thought that comes to you at the end of the day, when you are daydreaming or you are wishing that you could do this or that, that re-occurring image is the ***desire*** of your heart. What you haven't known is that God gives you the desire, because it is of the Father. So ask yourself, "What do you care about the most?" If after spending time with God, you are no longer reiterating your past, or your own personal issues, you are actually in a place of relative wholeness, you're walking with God; the desires that keep coming back are the key to your destiny.

If you give merit to your desires and dreams, you will begin to understand why you have ideas and concepts. What you are tasting is not the power of your creativity, it is the power of the age to come. In other words, you are reaching into the future, which is how God is going to be running earth. You are bringing that into the present, and that is why you have ideas and concepts that bug you about how things ought to be. You should always be under the tension of the ideal vs. the real in the area of your assignment. If you are not bothered about something that needs to be fixed; some wrong that needs to be right; some cause that needs to be a corrected; if something hasn't moved you, you are not yet in the place where God has got you engaged with your assignment (don't be discouraged, though, this book is giving you understanding). But once you start getting moved by something, you start to discover, that's part of the secret to what you are called to fix; because it bothers you. Zeal shows up in the area of your passion, in your assignment. When you begin to get that "this should not be" type of mentality, mark it because that is an area where God's disposition of you is rising up. The sense of justice is there.

So a lot of this comes down to understanding that you are fearfully and wonderfully made, and realizing that all work is sacred, and God can be glorified in each of the spheres. Like Caleb, you could then say, "Give me my mountain," and will leave the earth empty with the same proclamation that our Savior did, "I have glorified You down here on the earth by completing **the work** that You gave **Me** to do" (John 17:4, *AMP*; emphasis added by authors). There is an end-time anointing to do just that. We'll cover that in the next and final chapter.

♺♻

Now Take Your Mountain

"Now therefore give me this mountain, whereof the
LORD spake in that day; for thou heardest in that
day how the Anakims were there, and that the cities
were great and fenced: if so be the LORD will be
with me, then I shall be able to drive them out, as
the LORD said." Joshua 14:12

L et's conclude this book by discussing a prophetic word
that God recently released to the church, that if taught
and received with the wrong worldview, will miss the
mark once again for the transition for the church and God's
people. The prophetic word is "in these last days, God is raising
up an Elijah Generation," a generation that will have the spirit
of Elijah. The scriptures that support this prophetic word are
Matthew 11:14-16; Matthew 17:11-12; Luke 1:17; and Malachi
4:5-6. The meaning of this prophetic word is "like a mantle was
placed on Elijah for his assignment, mantles that once rested
on the saints of old are falling on God's people to complete
their assignments. As you recall, the mantle that fell on Elijah's
protégé, Elisha, resonated with so much power that as a band
of people were laying someone in his (Elisha's) grave, *"when the*
man was let down, and touched the bones of Elisha, he revived,
and stood up on his feet "(2 Kings 13:21). This is what lies ahead
for the serious believer.

Romans 1:16-17 says, *"For I am not ashamed of the gospel of Christ: for it is the power of God unto salvation to every one that believeth; to the Jew first, and also to the Greek."* We are not simply talking about a power to tell people that they need Jesus and then go to heaven, but a power that manifests itself through believers as the kingdom of God.

The thing we cannot miss is that the spirit that was on Elijah was for one distinct purpose and according to Malachi 4, it was to turn the hearts of the people back to God. In 1 Kings 18, Elijah has a showdown with the prophets of Baal. The people were confused about "the true God." So Elijah was ordained by God to demonstrate His superiority. However, verse 37 reveals the ultimate purpose of the showdown: *"Hear me, O LORD, hear me, that this people may know that thou art the LORD God,* ***and that thou hast turned their heart back again"*** (emphasis added by authors). Get this: God had already prepared their hearts for Him. He merely needed someone to demonstrate His superiority.

People of God, we MUST get this. His superiority surpasses healing the sick (medicine can do that) raising the dead (defibrillators can do that), and casting out demons (psychotherapy and antipsychotic drugs can do that). The world longs to taste the supernatural. That's why the Harry Potter and X-men series are so popular. As a renowned faith teacher stated, "the heart's hunger for the supernatural is deep-seated in humanity, regardless of nationality or background because the human being is the offspring of 'The miracle God.'"

However, the devil is cunning. These movies and others like them pervert and desensitize the supernatural. In Exodus, when Moses threw down His rod, the magicians echoed, *"What, what,"* as they threw down their rod. But consider what happened when Moses' rod swallowed up their rods. It got everyone's attention, particularly Pharaoh (the king and decision maker). Selah!

The end time manifestation of the kingdom is going to be a witness that is going to be relevant TO THE WORLD, where the world is, and this is the part that the church, particularly the signs and wonders people, have to get a hold of because God wants to do exploits in Egypt. By that I mean, He not only wants to do the supernatural where it is an awesome manifestation. He wants to do the supernatural where it is a natural manifestation.

We are called to influence the kings and decision makers occupying the tops of these mountains. They have to experience a level of God's power that is undeniable. What happens if we solve the problems in every arena of society where their magicians (experts) have failed? For example, while in your Wi-Fi zone, if your gift is in the business mountain, you pull out one of those tags containing a witty invention to relieve America of the multi-trillion dollar deficit it is facing. That would turn some hearts and according to the word their hearts are prepared to be turned.

The world doesn't want to hear another sermon. They are screaming much like Cuba Gooding did in "Jerry Maguire," 'show me the money.' They're saying "show me your God or who's your daddy?"

And God is waiting to show out, but He can't show out until you show up. Jesus said, *"Believe Me that I am in the Father and the Father in Me; or else believe Me for the sake of the [very] works themselves. [If you cannot trust Me, at least let these works that I do in My Father's name convince you]"* (John 14:11).

I think you are beginning to see the point. We think too small. God is playing this game at a higher level and the believer who develops His worldview, is in for the ride of his/her life.

Oh how we have misunderstood our Lord's heart when He said, *"We are not of this world"* (John 17:14). Consequently, many believers make the mistake of believing their mission in life is to get out of it. He was referring to this world's system—Babylon. Babylon is a system where Satan is the architect. As we've intimated previously, he has been trying for years to get God out of every arena of society through the mind molders that shape every nation. He wants to occupy the top of the mountains in every one of those spheres of influence (religion, family, education, media, arts and entertainment, government and business).

Jesus was telling us we are not **of** the world, but we are **in** the world and to do something about it. Instead, due to ignorance we've left Satan virtually uncontested. The invitation is for God's anointed to go back and reclaim what has been lost (Luke 19:10); to regain the influence God designed for us in **every** arena of life, not just in the church, for Colossians 1:15-20 says *"all things were created by him and for him."*

What are we to do? Take a snapshot of your life. If you are reaching heights or achieving a level of prosperity or success that is enviable, yet do not have your interior self—your soul in alignment, (i.e., you are still carnal, mean as a rattlesnake, envious, jealous, covetous, narcissistic, flaky, pitiful, etc.—you know—the heart knows its own bitterness), I would seriously examine whether this "success" is of God. Luke 4 says the devil promotes too. God's intense love for you would never allow you to ascend the mountain of career influence above what you are able to handle.

Here is something you probably don't think of, "it's a blessing not to be led into temptation." And that's exactly what the Lord's Prayer is covering, when He said pray "Lead me not into temptation." The translation can be read, "Keep me from any success, wealth, or increase that will expose me to the enemy where I can't handle him. Lead me not into a situation that succeeds to the point where my vulnerabilities—those areas I have not taken care of, are exploited and I end up getting taken out." Lead me not into temptation means God protects me from premature success. Remember Satan boasts of His ability to get almost anyone to bow the knee (to him).

If this is the case, take this book as an invitation from God to enter a level of training and preparation that will posture you for a life of fulfillment beyond your wildest dreams (Ephesians 3:20). When you miss destiny, you miss the one time gift of doing what you were created to do. You miss the fullness of God's invitation. *Personal Mastery* takes care of that.

It is God's desire to reveal the power of the age to come by raising up champions. These champions will have the God-given ability to draw out of their sphere a manifestation of the wealth that God has hidden. God's people must resolve in their own hearts that the global stage has been set so that nations can see the tangible reality of the kingdom and come under the Lordship of the Lord Jesus.

The only question that remains is, "What sphere of authority has God given you and how would you administrate it for the Kingdom of God if you had authority for God's will to be done on earth as it is in heaven in that sphere?"

Let Brother Caleb inspire and motivate you. Consider how many funerals he attended as all of the "unbelieving believers" died in the wilderness (Numbers 14:28-29; 2 Corinthians 4:4). Still, when it was all over, at the age of 85, he said, *"And now, behold, the LORD hath kept me alive, as he said, these forty and five years, even since the LORD spake this word unto Moses, while the children of Israel wandered in the wilderness: and now, lo, I am this day fourscore and five years old. As yet I am as strong this day as I was in the day that Moses sent me: as my strength was then, even so is my strength now, for war, both to go out, and to come in. Now therefore give me this mountain, whereof the LORD spake in that day . . .;"* (Joshua 14:10-12). He was saying, It doesn't matter that I am 85 years old, I've tracked with God, I've done my internal homework, I'm wired for it, I have the passion, the skills and the talent. Now give me my mountain.

No matter your age as you are reading this book, the disappointments life has *offered* you, and your erring in not knowing the scriptures, you are on the road to destiny as you embrace *Personal Mastery.* You my friend are a candidate for an invitation to join God in what He is doing. And His final word to you is, "Give me what I want and I will give you what you want."

Appendix
Testimonials

❧❧

Testimonials

As a child, I battled feelings of inferiority, depression, anger, and hopelessness, and with neither my mother nor my father being in the picture, and with me living with grandparents who resented my brothers and sister because we had to live with them, I contemplated suicide on more than one occasion. I was fearful though, because of everything I heard about suicide sending people to hell and all that stuff. So I never went through with it, and found refuge in Jesus. I never understood how I got to that place fully until I heard your teaching on EQ. I then began to understand how emotions and thoughts impacted my mental state, whether I was knowledgeable of them or not. I mean, I was a good kid. I never got into trouble or anything. I understand now how me not understanding about where I was mentally and emotionally regardless of what my surrounding might have been, guaranteed that I would have some sort of breakdown eventually. Prior to my step dad coming to get us from my grandmother's house, I contemplated killing my grandparents and then killing myself. Only God preserved me. Your teaching gave me so much clarity concerning the questions I had during that turbulent time in my life. I can't say that it saved my life because your teaching came much later, but I can honestly say that it did give me the Intel that I needed to ensure it would never happen again.

DM

The concept of EQ has helped me in my life immensely. I have always been an emotional being but unfortunately, it was in the negative way (or at least what I will deem as negative). I would hold in a lot of what I was thinking or feeling and not deal with it but instead brushing it off as if it didn't matter. In turn, this was damaging my heart and even tearing down my self-worth.

Once the EQ message was introduced to me, I began to manage my state so much better. I discovered that the emotions I was experiencing were real and that I had to deal with them if I wanted any personal success in my life. I realized that I could no longer ignore them as if they would go away but I had to deal with them in order to move forward.

Today because of greater understanding of managing myself and my emotions, I am able to pinpoint why I am feeling a certain way, where it came from and how to move forward.

AS

Before experiencing this teaching on EQ, I always knew that I was destined to live a prosperous life. The biggest question was "how?"

For my entire adult life, I thought that if you "put on a happy face," all would be well. Colloquially, this is known as "faking it until you make it." If you are honest with yourself, you will "make it" much quicker than if you "faked it." And that's *if* you even "make it" at all. Having a "happy face" is a small part of a larger problem. The larger problem is a negative thought process.

With more than 1,500+ words going through the human brain per minute, I had to examine how many of those words and thoughts were edifying and how many were detrimental to my emotional health. If I am not strong emotionally, it is nearly if not completely impossible for me to be emotionally strong for others. Through this teaching, I have learned that if there was ever a time to be real with myself, it would be now. Time waits for no one and I refuse to live a life that is anything other than prosperous. My question to you would be how do you plan to live a prosperous life without first having prosperous thoughts?

Because of this teaching, I am a firm believer that if you examine your thoughts, you will have the power to not only manage yourself but also the atmosphere around you. I have become a better wife, a better mother, a better employee and a better individual through this teaching and it is my hope that I am able to change others' lives with the experiences that have changed my own.

KD

What EQ has done for me, most importantly, is to make me aware of my thoughts and to discern where they are coming from. Additionally, to not allow the thoughts (if negative and not affirming) to linger long enough to become a part of me and produce behaviors that correspond with those thoughts. I have always been an internal thinker and tend to hold my thoughts in. I now understand that silent thoughts can hold you captive if you don't know what to do with them. The thoughts that I battled with were thoughts that I "thought" other people were having about me. It could have been because of a certain look or maybe I heard someone say something (that I perceived) was directed towards me or thoughts that because I was not invited to be close to a particular person or group of people, they felt that I was not good enough to belong. Those kinds of thoughts kept me captive for sooooo long. Now, I believe I understand that real or perceived, those thoughts could not have taken root unless I believed them to be true about myself.

Even as a wife and mother, there were times in the past, where I felt unappreciated and unneeded and I did have thoughts of what it would be like if I were not in the picture. There were thoughts of suicide, but never to the point of planning to execute suicide. I think it was more self-pity. The thoughts were intense enough that when I went there, it was as if all of the other negative thoughts about everything else in life followed and piled up to the point where it felt like an extreme attack. I really don't remember how I was able to escape the thoughts, but obviously, I was able.

Although some of my friends and family, members had a perception of me as always having it together or being very confident, I was not totally. I wasn't a train-wreck waiting to happen, but still those disempowering thoughts held me captive and kept me from growing forward.

Having negative thoughts about myself and not loving myself unconditionally didn't benefit me nor does it benefit anyone else that I am in relationship with. I think it is very contaminating.

The negative thoughts still come, but now I'm learning and practicing how to be aware of them, expose them and examine them and then put them in their place and make the adjustment.

It is empowering and freeing to have the information on EQ. When negative thoughts and feelings dominate your mind, it weighs you down and they are self-defeating and that is way too much power to give anyone or anything. If invited to remain, negative thoughts can be like quicksand, you will continue to sink deeper and deeper until you are destroyed. You will become the walking dead (living, but no quality of life) or it can get you to a place where you do want to commit suicide just as a way out. The way out is not suicide. The way out is by being empowered to be aware of your thoughts and feelings and not allowing them to have control over you and thus your behavior. The way out is to constantly be aware of them and when they are not in line, to make a choice to make the adjustment.

Life is too good and there is a future seeking to be manifested through me!

CC

Perry & Belinda Moss have done their internal homework resulting in the development of their authentic voice. Their words are thick and sticky—they leave a lasting impression on the hearts and minds of people.

You are guaranteed to enjoy their bold, no-nonsense approach. Their passion will ignite your zeal and your own passion for truth, wholeness, and God's word. Be prepared *to change.*

For teaching CDs or DVDs from them or to request their ministry gift at your church, seminar, or next conference, please call or write us at:

Repairers of the Breach Ministries
P.O. Box 911
Smithfield, VA 23431
(757) 356-9727
Or visit us on the World Wide Web at www.soteriacci.org